Upon the Pun

Dual Meanings in Words and Pictures

PAUL HAMMOND

and

PATRICK HUGHES

GREEN MAGIC

CW01465502

Upon The Pun © 2025 by Paul Hammond and Patrick Hughes.
All rights reserved. No part of this book may be used
or reproduced in any form without written permission
of the Authors, except in the case of quotations
in articles and reviews.

Green Magic
53 Brooks Road
Street
Somerset
BA16 0PP
England
www.greenmagicpublishing.com

Designed and typeset by Carrigboy, Wells, UK
www.carrigboy.co.uk

First published in 1978

ISBN 978 1 915580 29 0

GREEN MAGIC

To Ana Forcada
To Di Atkinson

Contents

Introduction

We wrote this book because we wanted to read it. No one else had written it, there has never been a clear and comprehensive study of verbal puns and double meaning, let alone visual puns and double meaning. Modern linguists have ignored this imaginative and widespread kind of word use. No art critic has ever developed a cogent theory of visual punning. We think that it is instructive to analyse the forms of verbal dual meaning and visual dual meaning, and that it is revealing to consider them side by side.

Paul Hammond and Patrick Hughes

Distinction between the Verbal Pun and the Play on Words

The excitement at the circus is in tents.

This **sentence** contains a **pun** on the word **intense**. Usually one sentence has one meaning. This sentence contains two meanings. One meaning is 'the excitement at the circus is intense'. The other is 'the excitement at the circus is in tents'. **In tents** sounds the same as **intense**, but has a different meaning. Words that sound the same, but are spelt differently, and have different meanings, are said to be homophonous (**homo** means '**same**', and **phono** means '**sound**'). **Intense** and **in tents** are **homophones**. A pun is made when someone notices that two different words sound the same, and constructs a sentence containing this sound. The two meanings of the sentence depend on the interpretation of the ambiguous sound.

An architect in prison complained that the walls were not built to scale.

This sentence contains a play on the word **scale**. There are two meanings here, each of which is expressed in exactly the same words. One meaning is 'an architect in prison complained that the walls were not built to scale (to climb)'. The other is 'an architect in prison complained that the walls were not built to **scale** (to

....
We who are about to sigh dilute you!

8

proportion)'. Words which sound the same, are spelt the same, but have different meanings, are said to be homonymic (**homo** means 'same', and **nym** means 'name'). **Scale**, 'to climb', and **scale**, 'to arrange in proportion', are **homonyms**. **Aplay on words** is made when someone notices that one word has two different meanings, and constructs a sentence containing this word. The two meanings of the sentence depend on the interpretation of the ambiguous word. (The play on words is also known as **double meaning**.)

The difference between the pun and the play on words is that in the pun completely different words, having completely different meanings, are noticed to have the same or similar sounds, and are brought together in one sentence; whereas in the play on words one word is noticed to have two meanings, which have diverged from one common root word, and these different meanings of the same word are brought out. In the examples quoted above **scale**, 'to climb', and **scale**, 'to arrange in proportion', are etymologically linked, coming from the Latin word **scala**, meaning 'ladder'. Obviously **in tents** and **intense** are not etymologically linked.

Both the pun and the play on words condense two meanings into one set of sounds: they are both useful to the journalist in composing headlines that encapsulate into a few words the more complex sense of a particular story. But they have different qualities. The pun starts with an accident of language; two different words happen to sound alike. Of course we often read puns, and all the puns in this book are written down, but punning depends on the sound of words: a sound links together two meanings. (Doctors forbid singers recovering from injured throats to read: even the sophisticated adult reader forms the words he is reading with his throat muscles.) The pun has a capricious and irrational quality.

....

If all the girls at this party were laid end to end, I wouldn't be at all surprised. (Dorothy Parker)

On the other hand the play on words is, because of the identical spelling of the different meanings, equally happy in speech or writing. The divergent meanings of one root word are reunited in the play on words. Thus the play on words has a rational, erudite quality.

....
What is the difference between a letter ready for posting and a lady going along a road?

TWO

The Double Entendre, A Kind of Double Meaning

The double entendre is a play on words one meaning of which is lewd:

Did you hear about the sleepy bride who couldn't stay awake for a second?

This sentence contains a play on the word **second**. One meaning is 'did you hear about the sleepy bride who couldn't stay awake for a second (moment of time)?'. The other is 'did you hear about the sleepy bride who couldn't stay awake for for a second (bout of lovemaking)?'. Since **second**, 'moment of time', and **second**, 'next after first', are etymologically the same, this is clearly a variety of the play on words.

One is addressed in an envelope and the other is enveloped in a dress.

THREE

Visual Equivalents to the Pun, the Play on Words, and the Double Entendre

Tomi Ungerer's picture (1) contains a **visual pun** on a dog's head. Usually a picture has a single reading. This picture has two readings. In one reading an armchair is seen as an armchair, in the other, it is seen as a dog's head. A visual pun is made when someone notices that two different things have a similar appearance, and constructs a picture making this similarity evident.

The design (2), an advertisement for an extractor fan, is a **visual double meaning**. There are two readings of this picture. In one reading an extractor fan is seen as an extractor fan; in the other, it is seen as a person's nose. There is no etymology in visual representation. We propose that the visual equivalent of etymology is **function**. This picture relates the function of a fan, to absorb smells, to the function of a nose, to perceive smells. It does not have the arbitrary quality of the pun, it has the rational quality of the play on words.

'Blimey – what a man!', a comic postcard (3), contains a visual double entendre. In one reading a fireman is directing a hoseful of water at a burning building. In the other, lewd, reading he is directing a stream of urine. The function of a hosepipe is here related to a function of a penis: to emit and direct water. In the verbal double entendre one word, of the same etymology, carries two meanings, one of which is lewd. In the visual double entendre one representation of a thing, having a common function, carries two meanings, one of which is lewd.

....

A girl's best friend is her mutter. (Dorothy Parker)

1. Tomi Ungerer, collage/drawing, from **Horrible**, 1960. Courtesy éditions Delpire, Paris

2. Anon, 'Vent-Axia ' collage/drawing, contemporary. Courtesy of Vent Axia Ltd., London

....
I've got a long felt want. (Eric Morecambe)

3. Fitzpatrick, 'Slimey — What a Man!', postcard, contemporary. By kind permission of Bamforth & Co. Ltd., Holmfirth, Yorks

FOUR

Homophones, Homonyms, and Etymology

To distinguish fully between a pun and a play on words it is necessary to have recourse to etymology, 'an account of the facts relating to the formation and meaning of a word' (O.E.D.).

> *Christopher Morley, seeing two wigs of the same small size in a shop window, concluded: 'They're alike as toupées.'*

This is a straight **homophonic pun**. There is no etymological relation between **toupées and two peas**.

> *Tired of listening to a lengthy plea for clemency towards a man condemned to hang, the judge said, 'I think we had better let the subject drop.'*

This is a straight **homonymic play on words**. Obviously **to drop the subject** 'conversationally', and **to drop the subject** 'literally', are of the same etymology. But consider:

> *The W.V.S. member who said she could thoroughly recommend a Mediterranean cruise for unaccompanied ladies. 'People,' she explained, 'should not believe all they are told. Sex orgies aboard ship are all bunk.'*

Bunk meaning 'bed' and **bunk** meaning 'nonsense' are homonyms, they are spelt the same. Yet they do not have the

....
For real enjoyment give me a well-boiled icicle.

same etymology. **Bunk** meaning 'nonsense' is an abbreviation of **bunkum**, itself a corruption of **Buncombe**, a county in North Carolina associated with its long-winded representative Felix Walker, who excused himself during one tedious oration in 1820 by saying that his electors expected him to 'make a speech for Buncombe'. **Bunk** meaning 'nautical bed' is a variant of **bunch**, in Middle English **bunche**, and comes direct from the Old Swedish **bunke** or Old Norse **bunki**, meaning 'heap' or 'pile'. Thus this rare case is a **homonymic pun**.

> *Bill meeting Mame on the street: 'What makes you walk so stiff, Mame?'*
> *Mame: "Cause I've got on patent-leather shoes, and patent-leather draws.'*
> *Bill: 'Oh, you have, eh?'*
> *Mame (indignantly): 'It does!'*

Drawers meaning 'a close undergarment for the lower limbs' and **draws** meaning 'causes to perspire' are spelt differently but sound the same, they are homophones. But they come from the same root **draw** meaning 'pull', 'haul', etc, deriving from Middle English **drawen**, which in turn derives from the Old English **dragan**, and so on. This rare case is a **homophonic play on words**. (Furthermore, since one of its meanings is lewd, it is a double entendre.)

....
Why is a hot summer's day like a very clear frosty night?

FIVE

The Continuum between the Visual Pun and the Visual Double Meaning

There are differences between words and pictures. Words can be read with the eyes or heard by the ears. This dual nature of words allows the pun to put sound before meaning, and permits the play on words to put meaning before sound. Pictures can only be seen. Since there is no parallel duality in pictures, there is a less clear-cut division between the visual pun and the visual double meaning, there is more a continuum.

'L'Amour de Pierrot', an Edwardian postcard (4), is a typical visual pun on a skull. In one reading Pierrot and his lady are seen making love, in the other the lovers' tryst is seen as a death's head. An arbitrary resemblance has been deliberately manufactured by the artist. The resemblance between, say, the feathery fan and the glasses of wine, and the teeth of the skull, is quite capricious, all the visual resemblances being of this order. This example stands at the arbitrary, irrational end of the continuum of visual play.

'A Little Fresh 'air from Selsey', a comic postcard (5), is closer to visual double meaning. It is a picture of a clay head with cress growing out of it. The two readings of the picture are of cress as cress and of cress as green hair. A somewhat rational resemblance has been played upon. Both hair and cress are thin and spiky and grow as a crop of very similar blades. This example stands at the rational end of the continuum of visual play.

....
Because it's the best time for seeing the grate bare.

4. Anon, 'L' Amour de Pierrot', postcard, c. 1905. Collection Patrick Hughes

5. Anon, 'A Little Fresh 'air From Canterbury', postcard, n.d. Collection Brian Mills

At the visual pun end of the continuum there is likely to be a greater degree of illusionism, necessary to make the arbitrary resemblances work. At the visual double meaning end of the continuum there is likely to be a lesser degree of illusionism because the resemblances shown have some kind of rational or functional basis already.

Is that a gun in your pocket, or are you just glad to see me? (Mae West)

SIX

Auditory shift in the Verbal Pun

Puns take liberties with language in various ways. Puns may have a greater or lesser degree of phonetic similarity. Hilaire Belloc wrote:

When I am dead, I hope it may be said,
His sins were scarlet, but his books were read.

Read sounds exactly the same as **red.** There is no phonetic shift. Jim Hawkins said:

There's a vas deferens between children and no children.

There is a difference between **vas deferens** and **vast difference.**

When punning goes further, it tends towards rhyme and assonance. Carolyn Wells'

Circumstances alter faces

revives the cliché by rhyming **faces** with **cases**. This is a **rhyming pun**. George S. Kaufman said:

One man's Mede is another man's Persian.

He renewed the proverb by making **Mede** assonant with meat, and **Persian** with **poison**. This is not aural illusion as in the pun proper, but aural assonance, an **assonant pun**. Kaufman also said

....
I've been things and seen places. (Mae West)

One man's meat is another man's poisson.

Another form of liberty-taking is the addition and subtraction of syllables. Carolyn Wells'

Every dogma must have its day

refurbishes the saying by adding **ma** to **dog**. When Saki said:

Beauty is only sin deep

he twisted the sense of the epigram by subtracting the **k** from **skin**.

....
What is the difference between a cloud and a whipped child?

SEVEN

Shifts in Illusion in the Visual Pun

Consider 'The Bald Breasts' **(6)**. There is a high degree of visual illusion here. Just as in the verbal pun the two words are encapsulated in one sound, in this visual pun the men's heads and the girl's breasts are encapsulated in the same pattern of marks.

In Sine's drawing **(7)** there is a lesser degree of illusion. As befits his situation the prisoner has more limited means at his disposal to create, by punning, the woman he desires.

Context becomes more important as the visual pun becomes less illusory. Take John Heartfield's photomontage **(8)**. The backside is made into a face solely by the addition of ears; the brains of his political enemies, Heartfield says, are in the seats of their trousers.

....

One pours with rain, the other roars with pain.

6. Anon, 'The Bald Breasts', postcard, c. 1905

....

When I told him he must clean off the mould he said there was
no must about it.

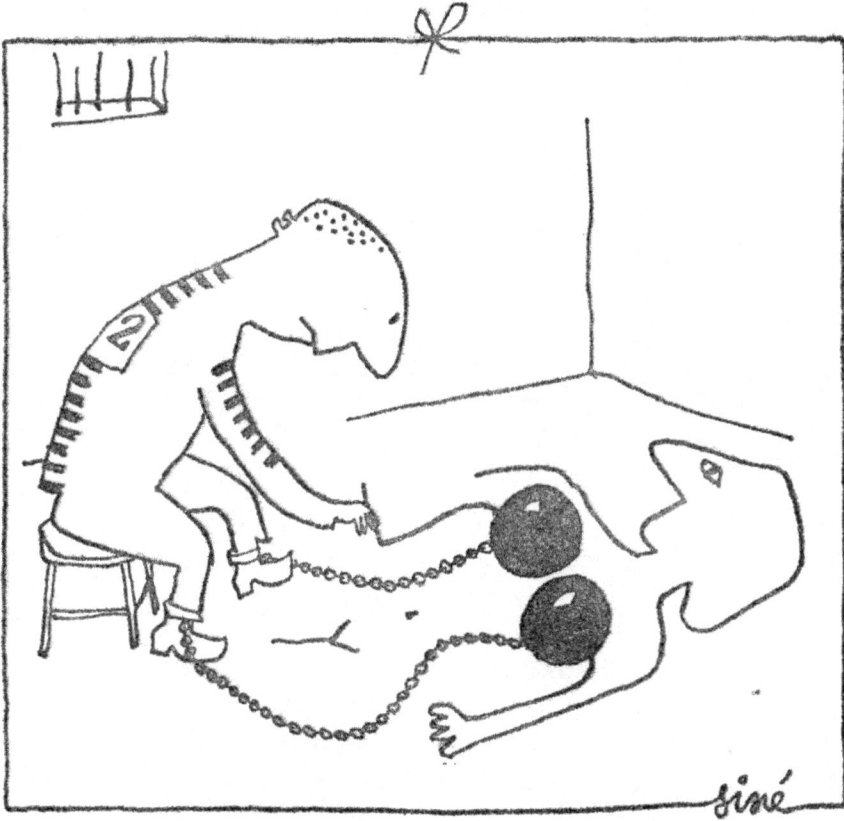

7. Sine, drawing from Bennett, The Best Cartoons From France, 1953. Courtesy Simon & Schuster, New York

That woman's a witch. I put a hand on her knee and she turned into a lay-by.

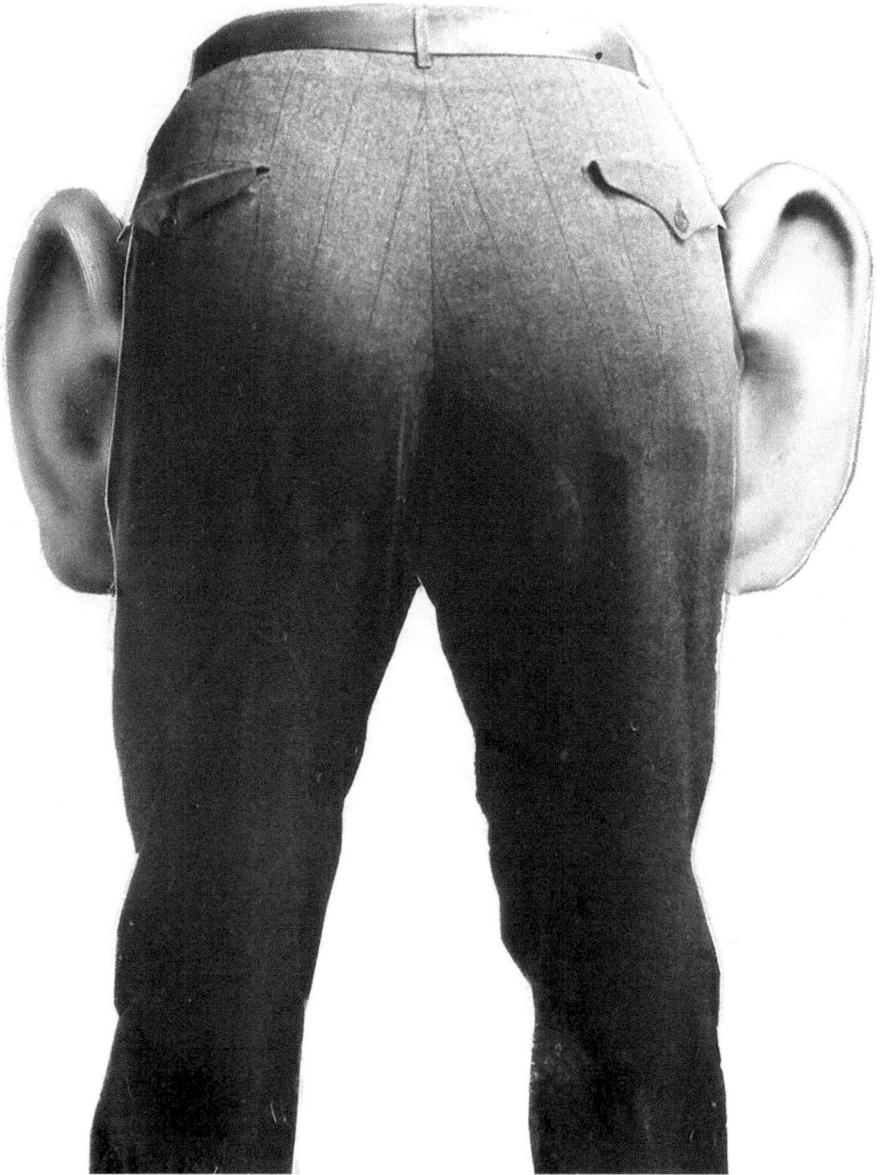

8. John Heartfield, 'Berliner Redensart', photomontage, 1928. Courtesy Frau Getrud Heartfield, Berlin

....

Q: Which has most legs, a cow or no cow?

EIGHT

Perceiving the Pun

All the verbal puns in this book are in print. We have had to decide which meaning to spell out and which to imply. In spoken punning of course the listener must decide for himself.

Similarly, when you see a visual pun one reading will register first. From fifteen feet, say, Arcimboldo's painting Water' **(9)** would seem to be a portrait head. From close to it is a pile of fish. Seeing this same picture in our book, the process is more open, or even reversed.

....
A: No cow has eight legs.

9. Giuseppe Arcimboldo, 'Water', oil painting, c. 1570. Courtesy Kunsthistorisches Museum, Vienna

NINE

Bathos and Cliché in the Verbal Pun

Nigel Vinson's pun

A wife's description of her husband: for whom the belle toils

operates at different levels. Death, alluded to in the original epigram, is a more profound subject than domestic drudgery. There is bathos here. It is in the pun 's nature to be bathetic, to be sublime and ridiculous all at once.

Why was Pharaoh's daughter like a shrewd, cold-blooded broker in a bear market?
It's because she got a handsome prophet from the rushes on the banks.

Religious leadership and mercantile shenanigans: bathos again.

Sometimes the two meanings of a pun are so trivial that they are balanced, they are both bathetic:

Is a lubricator someone who detests brick-built toilets?

On other occasions there is a near-perfect balance between the intensity of meanings in the pun:

Onlooker: "E don't 'arf make a row, mate!'
Proud father, holding baby boy: "E does that! 'E's got lungs like leather an' bawls like a bull!'

....

Ageing wife to husband: 'I'd like to do it tonight, but I'm afraid my back might peter out.'

Punning has another and opposite tendency: to shift a meaning in an upward direction. The pun often revitalises a cliché, proverb, or truism:

Any stigma will do to beat a dogma.

is attributed to Ronald Knox. E.W. Hornung, Arthur Conan-Doyle's brother-in-law, wrote:

Tho' he might be more humble,
There's no police like Holmes.

TEN

The Untangled Pun, Verbal and Visual

To understand one of the meanings of a pun you must mis understand the other.

> *A line of soldiers standing shoulder to shoulder were instructed to pass on the message, 'Send reinforcements, we're going to advance.' By the time the message had reached the end of a very long line the last soldier heard the order, 'Send three-and-fourpence, we're going to a dance.'*

This mis-hearing points up the essential in punning, that one set of sounds can carry two different meanings. Lewis Carroll described a similar situation:

> *I sit at the further end of the room; outside the door (which is shut) sits the scout; outside the outer door (also shut) sits the sub-scout; halfway down the stairs sits the sub-sub-scout; and down in the yard sits the pupil.*
>
> *The questions are shouted from one to the other, and the answers come back in the same way — it is rather confusing till you are well used to it. The lecture goes on something like this:*
> *Tutor: What is twice three?*
> *Scout: What's a rice tree?*
> *Sub-Scout: When is ice free?*
> *Sub-sub-Scout: What's a nice fee?*
> *Pupil (timidly): Half a guinea!*
> *Sub-sub-Scout: Can't forge any!*

....

Husband: 'My sentiments almost exactly!'

Sub-Scout: Ho for finny!
Scout: Don't be a ninny!
Tutor (looks offended, but tries another question): Divide a
hundred by twelve!
Scout: Provide wonderful bells!
Sub.-Scout: Go ride under it yourself!
Sub-sub-Scout: Deride the dunder-headed elf!
Pupil (surprised): Who do you mean?
Sub-sub-Scout: Doings between!
Sub-Scout: Blue is the screen!
Scout: Soup-tureen!
And so the lecture proceeds.

In this elaborate metamorphosis Carroll gives four sets of four alternative readings. He has shown how the listener can misunderstand words and put similar sounds with other meanings in their place. This is how the punster works: he asks of a word what other word that word might be.

Instead of condensing two meanings into one sound, there is a type of pun in which one sound is repeated twice; we call it the **untangled pun**:

Not a Trout there can be in the place,
Not a Grayling or Rud worth the mention,
*   And although at my hook*
*   With **attention** I look,*
*I can ne'er see my hook with **a Tench on**!*

Thomas Hood untangled this pun by giving both **attention** and a **Tench on**.

I never worry about diets. The only carrots that interest me are the number of carats in a diamond.

....
When is a girl like a mirror?

10. J.-J. Grandville, 'Going For a Walk in the Sky', engraving from **Un Autre Monde**, 1844

....

When she's a good looking lass.

Mae West's particular morality is not one of self-denial, it is one of bought favours, so she thinks of the number of carats in a diamond, not the number of carrots in a diet. The pun proper is like a metaphor, the untangled pun is like a simile.

Grandville's engraving 'Going For a Walk in the Sky' (10) is like Carroll's set of misunderstandings: the images change meaning with each transmission.

The Tern — The Turnip', a drawing by Robert Williams Wood (11) is an untangled visual pun. The visual punster notices resemblances and forces them to be exact. As far as Wood is concerned a tern is the same as a turnip.

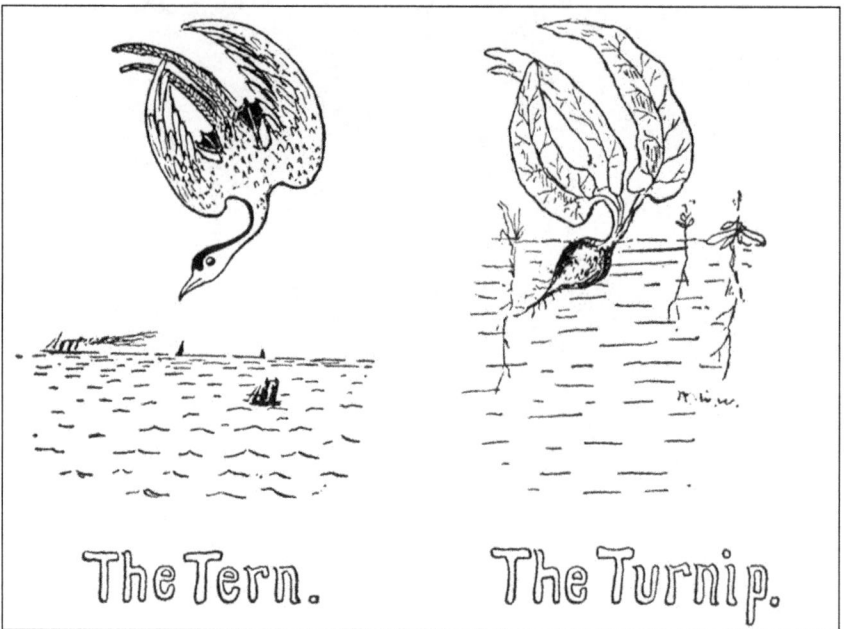

11. Robert Williams Wood, 'The Tern — The Turnip', drawing from **How to tell the Birds from the Flowers**, 1917

....
Why is a chrysalis like a hot roll?

ELEVEN

The Meld Pun, Verbal and Visual

When two words partially overlap, having one or more syllables in common, this is the **meld pun***:

Old people are inclined to fall into their anecdotage.

Thomas de Quincey overlapped **anecdote** and **dotage**, they share the common syllable **dote**. The meld pun makes a neologism:

Christmas is an alcoholiday.

There is a **visual meld pun**: one of our examples is prehistoric, the other is contemporary. An Aurignacian sculpture **(12)** overlaps two different readings. When seen from one side it looks like a woman with emphasised thighs and breasts; when seen from the other side it looks like an erect phallus.

*But see **portmanteau** word (pp73–74, 108)

....

Because it's the grub that makes the butter fly.

12. Palaeolithic sculpture

All his isms became wasms.

TWELVE

Etymological Shift in the Play on Words

To distinguish absolutely a play on words from a pun, it is necessary to look in an etymological dictionary to see whether the words played upon come from the same or from different roots. If they come from the same root it is a play on words; if they come from different roots it is a pun. But this is purely a formal definition of the distinction. How is the listener to know these etymological facts, as he hears a word-playing joke?

The best way for a woman to keep her youth is not to introduce him to other women.

In this play on words anyone would know that her youth, 'the state of her body', and her youth, 'the boy she possesses', come from a double meaning of the word youth.

An advertisement in the window of a chemist's shop read: WE DISPENSE WITH ACCURACY.

Here **dispense**, 'to dole out', and **dispense**, 'to do away with', come from a play on the same word, but not so obviously. In Anthony Earnshaw and Eric Thacker's dedication of their book **Wintersol**,

To the meek
who will inherit the earth
only by forging the will

....

She offered her honour; he honoured her offer; and all night long it was honour and offer.

forging the will, 'to become determined', and **forging the will**, 'to interfere with a legal document', come from an even less obvious double meaning. **Forging the will**, in the metaphorical sense of 'forming one's intentions in the white heat of rebellion', and **forging the will** in the sense of 'altering the figures on one's grandfather's bequest', do not immediately seem to have come from the same root meaning. On the other hand, **will**, 'your intention when dead', and **will**, 'your intention as a social group', can be seen quite clearly as a play on words. In fact **forging**, 'cheating', and **forging**, black- smithing', can be seen to be related in that both are operations to alter things in a precise way: their meanings have a common etymology in the Latin **fabricare**, 'to make, fabricate'.

From these examples it can be seen that there is a continuum from absolute clarity about the double meaning of the words played upon, a certainty of their identical etymology, to an area where it is possible to intuit or vaguely understand that the same root meaning is being taken in two ways. At the far end of this continuum there are examples which are plays on words but which no normal person could be expected to understand as being double meaning.

> *When is a schoolmaster like a man with one eye?*
> *When he has a vacancy for a pupil.*

No one would ever guess that **pupil**, 'scholar', and **pupil**, 'centre of the eye', share a common root **pupilla**, Latin for 'a child, especially an orphan, in the charge of a guardian or tutor', whence the sense of 'young scholar', since **pupilla** also designated in Latin the pupil of the eye, so named because of the tiny image reflected there. If one does not know, readily or by intuition, that a word is being used in two related senses, it might just as well be an accident of sound or spelling that links the two meanings, it might just as well be a homonymic pun.

....

More waist, less speed (David Walters)

THIRTEEN

Functional Shift in the Visual Double Meaning

Visual double meaning extends from where the things played upon share very similar functions, to where the relation between the things played upon is functional at different levels, allegorical or symbolical. In Salvador Dali's illustration (13) the breasts of two doves stand for the two breasts of a woman. This is a transparently double meaning, breasts stand for breasts.

Millais used a similar double meaning, probably unconsciously, in his picture 'The Return of the Dove to the Ark' (14).

Dürer, in 'The Men's Bath' (15), made a play on a faucet and a penis: they share the function of emitting water.

In Jane Graverol's painting 'The Spirit of Water' (16) the two functions being played upon are somewhat different, at least in scale. Water rushes from a gorge, and water rushes from a bottle. It is the function of a bottle to contain liquid, and it so happens that a gorge may too.

Arcimboldo's librarian' (17) is made up of the tools of his trade. The remark, what a man does is what he is, is given figurative form. His magnifying glasses have become his eyes, book-markers have taken the place of his fingers. This is visual double-meaning at an allegorical level.

....
Monogamy leaves a lot to be desired. (A.F.G. Lewis)

13. Salvador Dali, lithograph from Sandoz, **The Maze**, 1945. © by A.D.A.G.P.,
Paris

14. John E. Millais, detail from 'The Return of the Dove to the Ark', oil painting, 1851. Courtesy Ashmolean Museum, Oxford

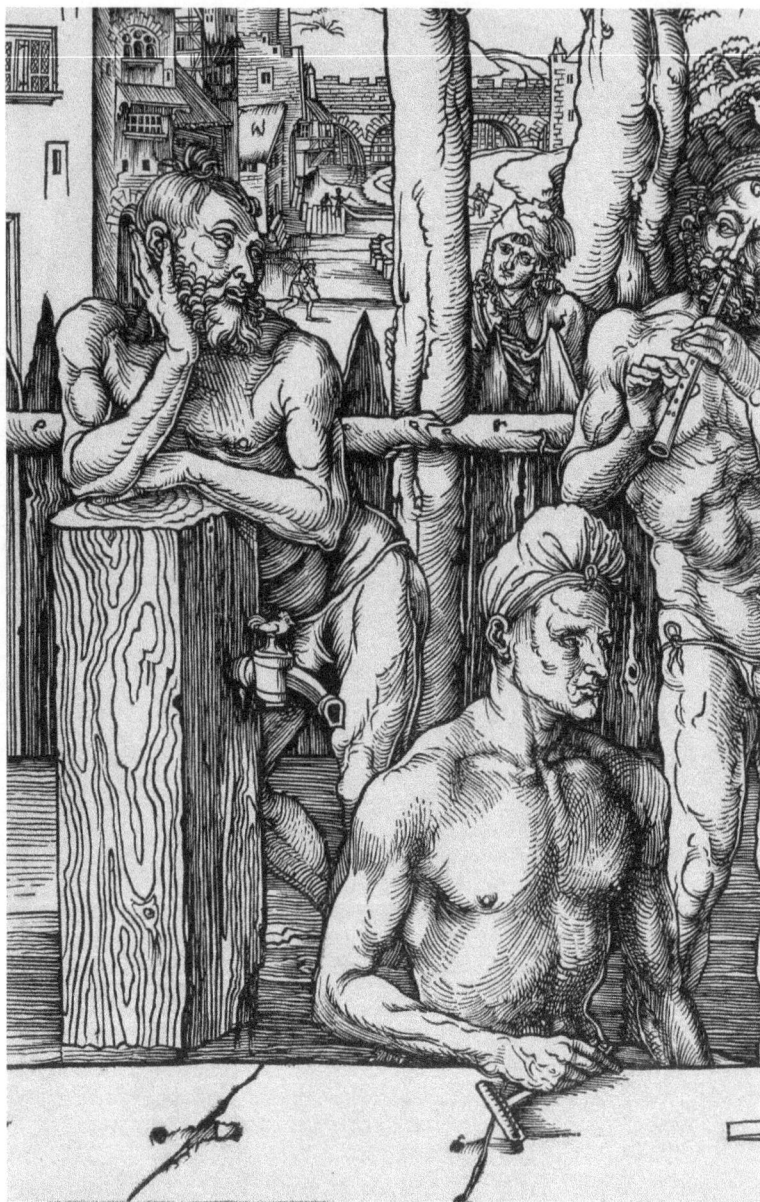

15. Albrecht Dürer, detail from 'The Men's Bath', woodcut, c. 1497

16. Jane Graverol, 'The Spirit of Water', oil painting, 1959

17. Giuseppe Arcimboldo, 'The Librarian', oil painting, 1563. Courtesy of Svenska Portrattarkivet, National-Museum, Stockholm

....

Minister of War: Sir, you try my patience.

FOURTEEN

The Technique of the Verbal and Visual Double Entendre

One way of exploiting sexual inhibition is the double entendre:

> *A messenger boy delivers flowers to an actress, naked in her dressing room, and stays to stare.*
> *'Run along now,' she says, giving him a tip, hear somebody coming.'*
> *'You have marvellous hearing,' he says. 'That's me.'*

Many of the words and phrases used in ordinary language have other meanings in talk about sex. We all know that **coming** means 'arriving', but it also means 'ejaculating'. In the double entendre the lewd meaning can only be understood by someone who understands lewd meanings.

There is a mechanism known to naughty children for investing the most banal remarks with another, sexual meaning. The unwitting parent might say, of a suitcase that he has put on the back seat of the car, 'I've got it in but it's fallen off.' The child will add, '… as the actress said to the Bishop!' Thus the adult's ordinary statement is placed in the context of eroticism.

> *A highly respectable lady was asked by a messenger if she had no letter to give him for her husband, who had been abroad for some time as Ambassador of the Republic. 'How could I write,' said she, 'since my husband has taken away the pen, and left the inkstand empty?'*

....

Firefly, (Groucho Marx): I don't mind if I do. You must come over and try mine sometime.

18. Thomas Rowlandson, 'Stolen Kisses', lithograph, c. 1815

When Poggio's words **pen** and **inkstand** are taken lewdly, they operate at a metaphorical level. Symbolically, writing a love letter is compared to making love.

> *I suppose I should tell you about Lord Redding's recent marriage to a woman some forty years younger than himself. The London Times account of the wedding ended, unfortunately, with this sentence: 'The bridegroom's gift to the bride was an antique pendant.'*

Alexander Woollcott perceived the double entendre in this innocuous report.

....

See nipples and die. (M. Levine)

19. Quip, 'Just Married', postcard, contemporary. Courtesy of D. Constance Ltd., Littlehampton

Function in the visual double entendre is literally related to bodily function. A good example is Thomas Rowlandson's 'Stolen Kisses' (18). The old man happens to stand in front of a cannon such that the gun's barrel stands for his erect penis, a reading fortified by other details. His pretty girl is canoodling with a young sailor; the cover of his tumescent telescope drips down; a pile of unused cannon balls stand behind him. The penis and the cannon share a similar appearance, and function; they both go off with a bang.

In Quip's seaside postcard (19) one reading of the groom's shadow is of a man holding a tube of toothpaste, the other is of a man with an enormous erect penis. The artist has noticed that shadows can be ambiguous, and links two meanings in the shadow.

....

Anxious theatregoer trying to bustle past novice usher: 'But I have a mezzanine box!'

FIFTEEN

Generality, Metaphor, Contradiction and Adianoeta in the Play on Words

When two words share a common etymology the link between them will be formed by generality or metaphor.

A good job in the winter is selling newspapers: each copy sold increases circulation.

Here **circulation** can mean both 'circulation of the blood' and 'cir- culation of a newspaper'. **Circulation** is a sufficiently general word that it can be used in more than one sense.

When Marilyn Monroe was asked if she had anything on when she posed for some calendar shots, she replied, 'The radio!' or 'Chanel No. 5!'

Again, this play on the word **on** is possible because, like **circulation**, **on** is a word of general use which can have different meanings in different contexts.

Another major way plays on words are formed is to take metaphors literally:

Q: Why did the French revolutionaries win?
A: Because the aristocracy lost their heads.

....

Usher: 'Lady, I don't care if you have brass tits. Keep to the right!'

Language abounds with dead metaphors — **dead** itself is a dead metaphor — and plays on words remind us of the metaphorical basis of much of our language.

It isn't safe to sleep in trains because trains run over sleepers.

The wooden supports under railway lines are called sleepers because they just lie there. It is a metaphor to call them sleepers, they were never awake.

The irrationality of the pun is expressed in bizarre chance absurdities:

Minister of War: Gentlemen, gentlemen! Enough of this. How about taking up the tax?
Firefly (Groucho Marx): How about taking up the carpet?
Minister of War: I still insist that we must take up the tax.
Firefly: He's right. Y ou've got to take up the tacks before you take up the carpet.

The play on words, being a more rational form, erudite and etymologically sound, tends to express its irrationality in downright contradiction:

Q: Why is an empty room like a room full of married people?
A: Because there isn't a single person in it.

One of the ways the play on words achieves logical contradiction is by taking literally a verbal usage which is operating at some other level.

Q: Why didn't the man who walked three miles get very far?
A: Because he only moved two feet.

This play on the word **foot** meaning 'twelve inches' takes literally the usage of **foot** as a measure of distance, a practical metaphor,

....
Why are birds melancholy in the morning?

which refers to the time when men measured distance by pacing it out.

A subtle kind of logical contradiction in the play on words is the rhetorical form **adianoeta**, which means 'not noticed'. For example:

> *A critic says to a good friend who is also a poor novelist, 'I will lose no time in reading your new book.'*

The friendly critic is paying a back-handed compliment in saying both that he will hurry to read the book and that he will not waste his time reading the book.

> *A publisher once said to two authors, 'For your work, Hammond and Hughes, I have nothing but praise.'*

....

Because their little bills are all over dew.

SIXTEEN

The Philosophical Distinction between the Pun and the Play on Words

THE PUN

While particular puns have particular meanings, punning as an activity exemplifies certain attitudes and general meanings.

> *There was a man in a house and he could not get out. The only furniture was a table. He rubbed his hands until they were sore. Then he sawed the table in half. Two halves made a whole. He shouted through the hole until he was hoarse, jumped on the horse and rode away.*

The accidents of language have invested words like **sore** and **saw** with the same sound. The punster notices this accident of language, draws two disparate meanings together in each punning word, and orchestrates these absurd relations into a capricious whole.

The puns that free language free the man. Puns remind you that words are one thing and things are another, that **horse** is a word, but a horse is a horse. The punster finds words that sound the same, and makes relations between the things the words describe, which may be as different as anything.

....

May I sew you into a sheet?

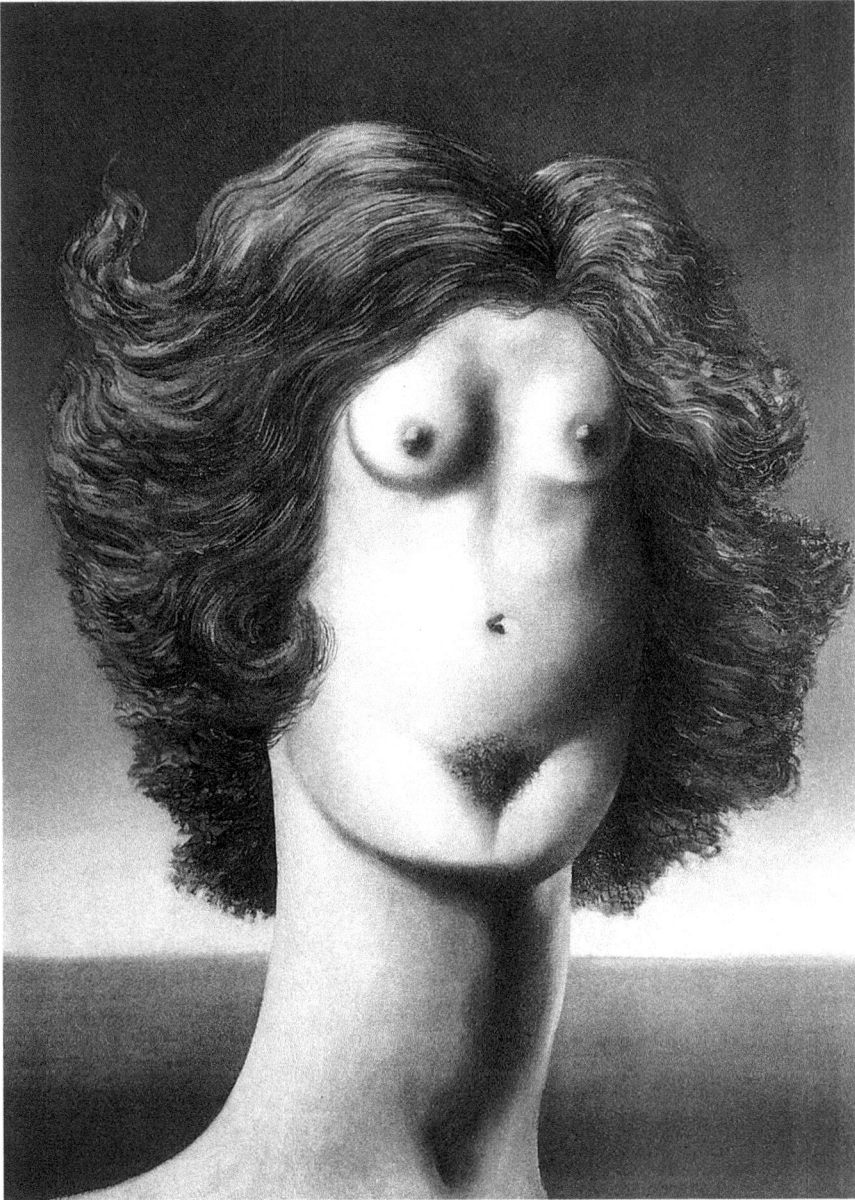

20. René Magritte, 'The Rape', oil painting, 1934

The cook was a good cook, as cooks go; and as cooks go she went. (Saki)

21. Anon, advertisement for paper, contemporary

....

How do girls get minks?

René Magritte's 'The Rape' **(20)** is a pun on a woman's head in which the features of her torso stand for the features of her face. The idea of seeing through one's nipples, or suckling at the eye, is startling. Imagine blowing your navel.

The visual pun reminds you that the representation of reality is the re-presentation of reality in another form, eg. oil on canvas, by representing two things at once, whereas in reality one thing is at once.

By presenting one set of marks in which you can see two things, the visual pun always refers to our ability to see things in things.

THE PLAY ON WORDS (DOUBLE MEANING)

Observing two housewives screaming at each other across a courtyard, Sydney Smith remarked that they would never agree because they were arguing from different premises.

Premises, 'logical propositions', and **premises**, 'buildings and adjuncts', share a common etymology in the Latin **praemittere**, 'to send before'. Smith makes a rational link between arguing across beliefs and arguing across territory. The meanings of **premises**, have diverged over the years from a common origin; Smith has brought them back together again, converged them. A major element in the philosophy of the play on words is its rationality: it rationalises the history of language.

In a contemporary advertisement **(21)** the mouthpiece of a telephone has been made into an ear. The mouthpiece has become the ear it leads to, the two things have converged.

Time flies, you cannot; they fly so fast.

This inscrutable epigram notes the common etymology of **time flies**, 'continuing existence passes quickly', and **time flies**, 'to

....
The same way minks get minks.

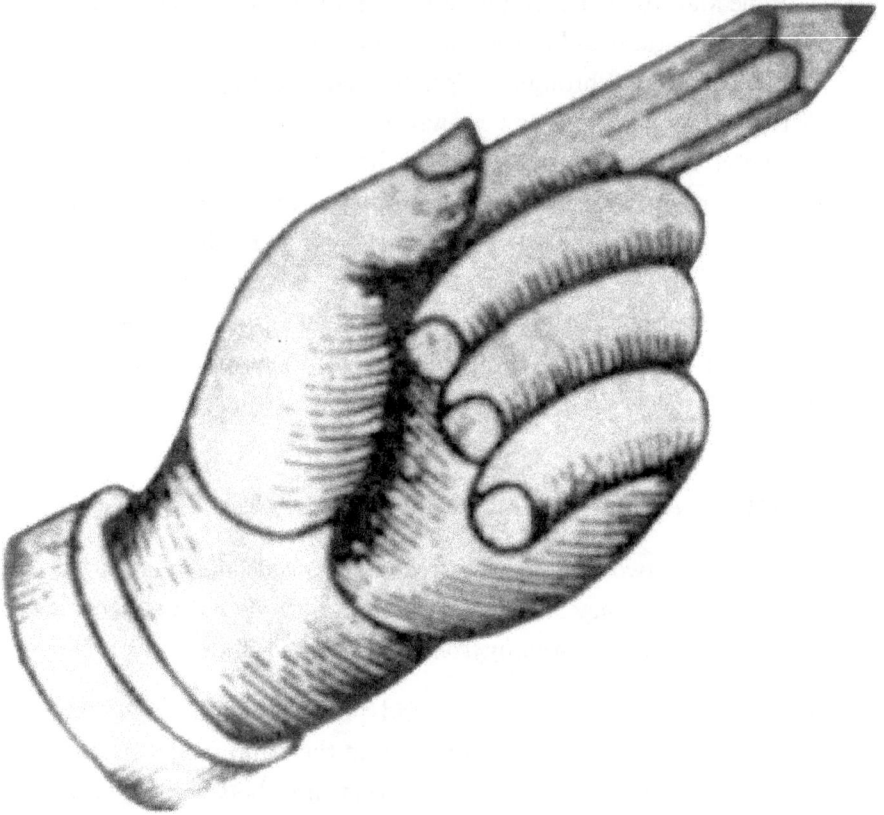

22. Anon, bookjacket illustration, 1974. Courtesy Cornell University Press, Ithaca, New York

measure the rate of movement of winged insects', in the Old English **tima**, meaning 'time', and in the Old English **fleogan**, meaning 'to fly'. The knowing or intuitive erudition characteristic of the play on words makes every man an etymologist.

Consider the drawing (22), which represents a finger sharpened to form a pencil. The finger has become that which it wields. We are referred back to a primitive function of the finger, to draw with pigment or make marks on soft surfaces. This is a kind of erudition about past and present functions of things.

....

What is the difference between a cat and a comma?

While the pun emphasises perception, the play on words emphasises cognition. In the pun, something can become something else if the things punned upon can be related by sound or by sight. In the play on words something can only become something else if it is like it in the first place, if the things played upon are related by etymology or by function.

....

A cat has its claws at the end of its paws and a comma has its pause at the end of a clause.

SEVENTEEN

Chiasmus and Metathesis

There are other forms in which words or images perform double duty. These are notably **chiasmus** and **metathesis**. Mae West said:

It's not the men in my life that count — it's the life in my men.

This is a chiasmus, which means 'crossing'. In a chiasmus two phrases are juxtaposed; the order of the words in the first is reversed in the second. Thus the words are crossed over; the focal words do double duty. In the first phrase **life**, 'Miss West's existence', has a different meaning to **life**, 'her boyfriends' virility', in the second phrase.

What is the difference between photography and the whooping-cough?
One makes facsimiles, the other makes sick families.

This is a metathesis, which means 'transposition'. In a metathesis words in a phrase exchange some of their letters to form new words in a new phrase. Here the words were **fac similes** and **sick families**. Swapping over the **fa** from **fac** to the **miles** of **similes** gave **families,** and the **si** from **similes** joined on the **c** from the end of **fac** to form **sick**.

The metathesis is like a pun, in that it deals in chance resemblances of sound between words. The chiasmus is usually like a play on words, in that it deals in the diverging meanings of a word.

....

The fact that people and trees and elephants and cars all have trunks just proves that there are more things than there are words. (Anon, Jr)

EIGHTEEN

Visual Chiasmus and Visual Metathesis

Just as in verbal language there are forms which transpose words or syllables to give a new meaning, there are examples in visual language of the transposition of images to give new meanings.

René Magritte's **Maternity (23)** is a **visual chiasmus**. In a verbal chiasmus the order of the words in the first phrase is swapped over in the second: in this visual chiasmus the heads of the mother and child are grafted onto the wrong bodies. The child is the mother of the man. (All images appear upside-down on the eye's retina. By the time they reach consciousness they are the right way up. The nerve which transmits the information from eye to brain is called the chiasmic nerve).

Illustration **(24)** is a frame from a comic strip by Gustave Verbeek called **The Upside-Downs of Little Lady Lovekins and Old Man Muffaroo.** Looked at one way up you see Old Man Muffaroo in a canoe threatened by the lashing tail of a fish, just as he reaches a small grassy knoll with two trees. The other way up you see Little Lady Lovekins held by the skirt in the beak of a Roc. This is an example of **visual metathesis**: parts of this picture become other things when inverted. In chiasmus entities, not details, are transposed. In metathesis fragments of words and things are changed in meaning as they change order: the foliage of the trees become the grass of the ground; the tree trunks become the Roc's legs; the land becomes the Roc's body; the fish becomes the head of the Roc; the canoe becomes the Roc's beak; and Old Man Muffaroo becomes Little Lady Lovekins.

....

He is the very pineapple of politeness! (Mrs Malaprop)

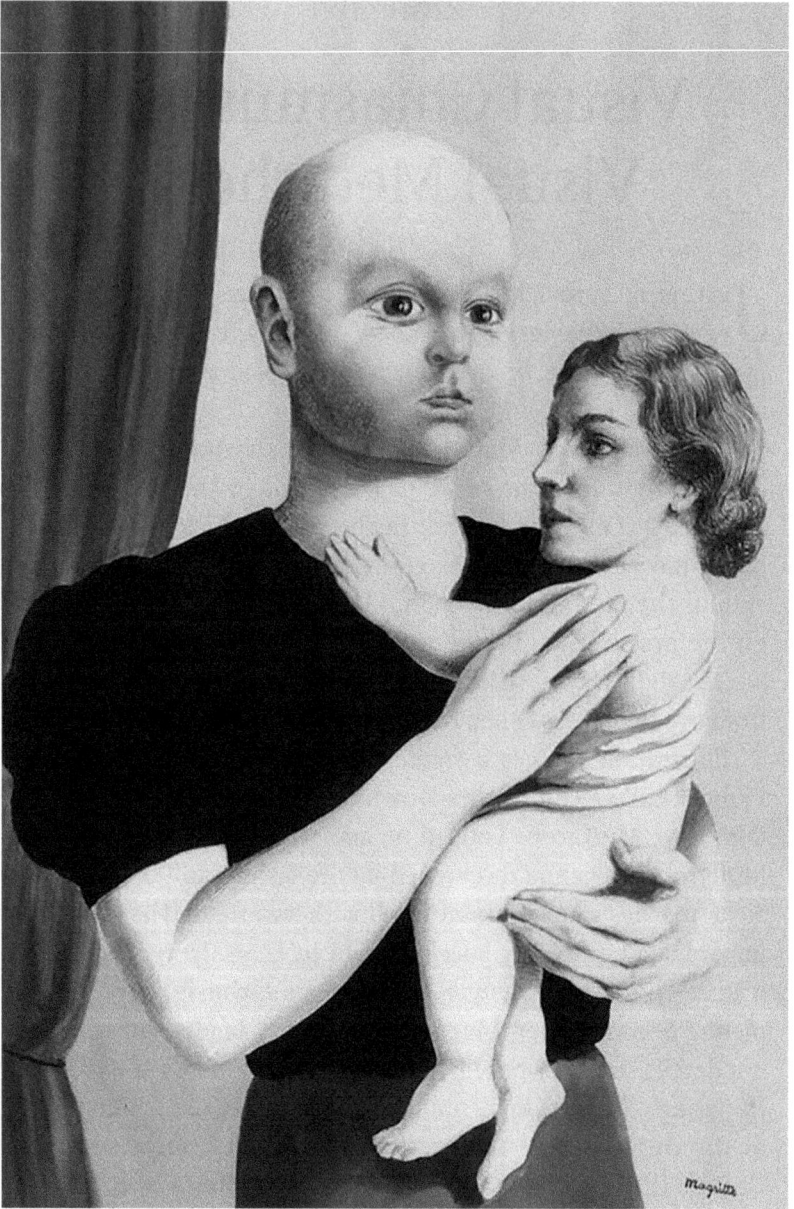

23. René Magritte, 'Maternity', watercolour & gouache, c. 1935

....

Why do widows wear black garters?

24. Gustave Verbeek, frame from comic strip, 1903–5

In memory of those who have passed beyond.

NINETEEN

Implied and Punning Chiasmus

An **implied chiasmus** was made by George Jean Nathan who, disturbed by the capacity of some actors to criticise their colleagues, said, 'Let him who is without sin, stone the first cast.'

Here Nathan merely implies the phrase **cast the first stone**. Dorothy Parker gave her reason for not meeting a deadline:

'Tell the editor I've been too fucking busy — or vice versa.'

While we have described chiasmus as being allied to the play on words, there sometimes is **punning chiasmus**.

The difference between a sewing machine and an illusion is that one sews seams and the other seems so.

Here whole words are transposed, **sews seams** becomes **seems so**, but the relation between **sew** and **so** and **seam** and **seem** is a punning one.

Groucho Marx, on entering a restaurant where a previous wife was present, said, 'Marx spots the -ex.'

X marks the spot is implied; **marks** and **Marx** and **-ex** and **X** are puns: this chiasmus is both implied and punning.

....

What is the difference between an angry circus owner and a Roman hairdresser?

Implied Metathesis, the Spoonerism and the **Contrepèterie**

George S. Kaufman's daughter once informed him that a friend of hers from Vassar had eloped. He remarked philosophically, 'Ah! She put her heart before the course.'

Here the wit implied the phrase **cart before the horse**; this is **implied metathesis**. The spoonerism and the **contrepèterie** are varieties of implied metathesis.

In everyday discourse people often accidentally transpose syllables between pairs of words, or even whole words. One man said to have perpetrated these errors at the hop of a drat is the Reverend W.A. Spooner (1844–1930). (Spooner, an albino, may have been the model for Carroll's White Rabbit.) Such accidental, or pseudo-accidental, metatheses have since been called **spoonerisms**. In a speech of welcome to Queen Victoria he is said to have said:

I have in my bosom a half-warmed fish.

Some spoonerisms result in nonsense. Spooner announced the hymn in church as:

Kinquering Congs Their Titles Take.

Some spoonerisms result in pun-sense. It has been observed that

it is easier for a camel to pass through the knee of an idol ...

....

One is a raving showman and the other is a shaving Roman.

This spoonerism, since it has a lewd meaning, is akin to a further variety of metathesis, the **contrepèterie**:

The pasta was missing before the fire darting.

By transposing the initial letters between pairs of words this sentence can be given the scatological meaning, **the master was pissing before the dire farting.** The game of **contrepèterie** has been popular in France since the twelfthcentury.

A visual analogy to the **contrepèterie** is the 'droodle' which presents one innocuous representation and one lewd one **(25).** This schematically represents a light bulb, but when inverted it turns into a naked lady bending over.

25. Anon, 'Light bulb/lady', drawing n.d.

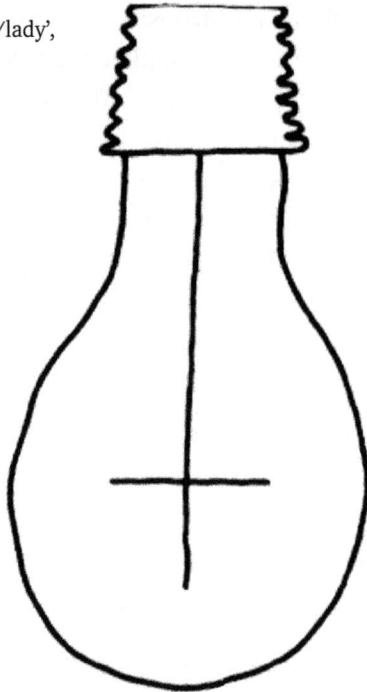

Why is life like a shirt-button?

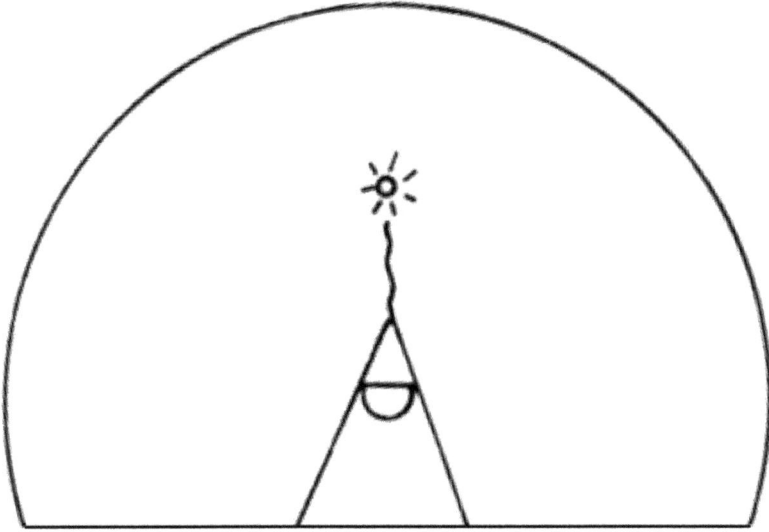

26. Anon Tepee/man', drawing, n.d.

A class is drawing a progressive picture on the blackboard, each child explaining what the picture represents at the step he has drawn. One draws a straight line representing the horizon, the second draws an Indian tepee on this horizon, the third a half-moon decoration near the top of the tepee, the fourth a wisp of smoke rising from the top, the fifth makes a small circle higher up representing the sun, and the sixth draws a set of rays all around the sun. Seventh is the bad boy. He says he doesn't know what to make of it, but it looks to him (drawing a large half-circle over the whole thing, beginning and ending at the horizon) like his father washing out the bathtub on a Saturday night.

As the naughty boy adds his half-circle to the picture (26) he changes its context completely, just as the images made to be inverted are given a new meaning when turned upside-down.

....

Because it only hangs by a thread.

TWENTY-ONE

The General Meaning of Chiasmus and Metathesis

The maker of chiasmus and metathesis has the inclination to turn things the other way round, to turn things inside out, to make them do double duty. This temperament to invert and transpose things is often met with in children, who might speak 'backward slang'; in an artist like Magritte, who transposed the usual arrangement of a mermaid (27); or in a humorist like Oscar Wilde who said that:

> work is the curse of the drinking classes.

The philosophy of chiasmus and metathesis is inherent in the technique. As things are literally turned inside-out or upside-down, the implication is either that 'when things are turned upside-down, what difference does it make?'; or, 'things are upside-down to begin with and this is a way of putting them to rights.' In **Alice in Wonderland**, Lewis Carroll speculated about these implications:

> 'You should say what you mean,' the March Hare went on.
> 'I do,' A lice hastily replied; 'at least — at least I mean what I say — that's the same thing, you know.'
> 'Not the same thing a bit!' said the Hatter. 'Why, you might just as well say that "I see what I eat" is the same thing as "I eat what I see"!'
> 'You might just as well say,' added the March Hare, 'that "I like what I get" is the same thing as "I get what I like"!'

....

What's the difference between a conundrum and a man's aunt who squints?

'You might just as well say,' added the Dormouse, which seemed to be talking in its sleep, 'that "I breathe when I sleep" is the same thing as "I sleep when I breathe"!'

Carroll progressively widens the gap of meaning between each statement and its inversion. This symmetry is enjoyable in itself.

When the terms of a chiasmus are quite abstract the result is close to logical contradiction. Marx, who often used chiasmus, wrote:

The weapon of criticism cannot, of course, replace criticism by weapons.

And Montaigne said:

A man who fears suffering is already suffering from what he fears.

This is the meeting place of wordplay and philosophy.

Because chiasmus is related to the play on words, it tends to share its philosophy:

All values are relative, but some relatives are better value than others.

Here we have the rationality, convergent thinking, and etymological erudition characteristic of the double meaning. The metathesis is a more atomic technique which attacks words, breaks them up into smaller parts, and reconstructs them.

What's the difference between a mouse and a young lady?
One wishes to harm the cheese, the other to charm the he's.

This is closer to the pun, the relation between young ladies and cheese is **arbitrary,** strange, and absurd.

Arcimboldo's 'The Peasant' **(28)** is a visual metathesis, in which a bowl of vegetables becomes a portly peasant. Perhaps

....

One is a query with an answer; the other an aunt, sir, with a queer eye.

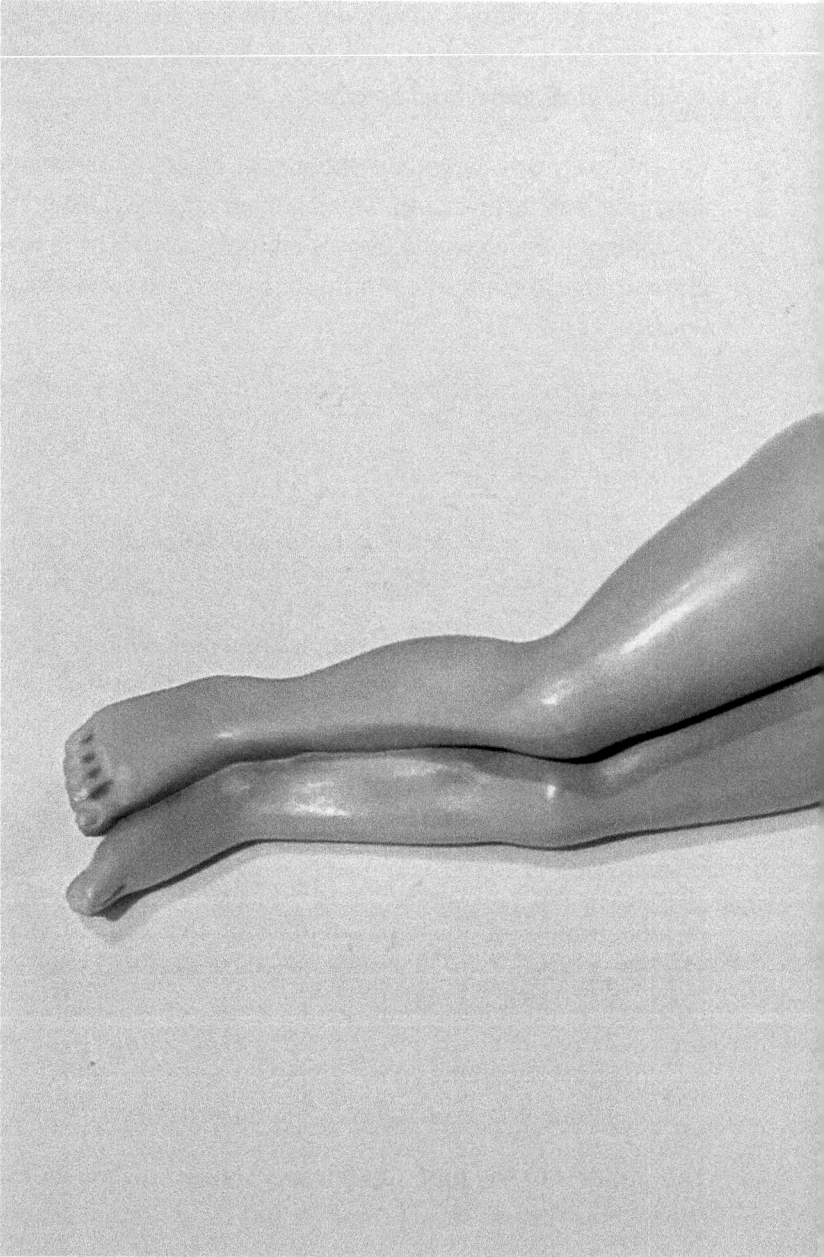

27. Mermaid sculpture after Réné Magritte, a visual chiasmus.

Your teeth are like stars: they come out at night.

Police to meet you.

28. Giuseppe Arcimboldo, 'The Peasant', oil painting, c. 1570. Courtesy Biblioteca Statale, Cremona

this painting hung on a wall above a table on which lay a mirror. The spectator first saw the painting of the vegetables, then looked down at the mirror and saw to his surprise the peasant. The use of a mirror points up the philosophy of visual inversion: that an image of the world one way round has as much coherence as the other way round.

TWENTY-TWO

The Malapropism, the Howler, the Portmanteau Word, the Holorhyme, the Homophonic Couplet, the Conundrum, the Riddle, Zeugma, the Wellerism, the Tom Swifty

A **malapropism** is when an ignorant person pretends to learning and can only express his ignorance. The malapropism is named after Mrs Malaprop in R.B. Sheridan's play **The Rivals** (1775):

'She's as headstrong as an allegory on the banks of the Nile.'

Mrs Malaprop wanted to say **alligator** but used a similar sounding word instead.

The malapropism is older than Mrs Malaprop. The Greeks called it **acyron**, the Romans **improprietas**, Puttenham, the sixteenth century English rhetorician, called it **uncouthe**. In **Much Ado About Nothing** Shakespeare wrote:

'O villain! thou wilt be condemn'd into everlasting redemption for this.'

Just as the spoonerism is a slip of the tongue, so the malapropism is a slip of the vocabulary. When such solecisms are committed by the young, they are called **howlers** or **boners**.

Britain has a temporary climate.

Sometimes howlers are merely based on bad spelling, which is a kind of unconscious punning:

In some buses they have smoking aloud.

A conscious use of the malapropism was made by Lewis Carroll in 'The Mock Turtle's Story':

> 'I couldn't afford to learn it,' said the Mock Turtle with a sigh, 'I only took the regular course.'
> 'What was that?' enquired Alice.
> 'Reeling and Writhing, of course, to begin with,' the Mock Turtle replied; 'and then the different branches of Arithmetic — Ambition, Distraction, Uglification and Derision.'
> (…)
> 'Well, there was Mystery,' the Mock Turtle replied, counting off the subjects on his flappers, — 'Mystery, ancient and modern, with Seaography: then Drawling — the Drawling-master was an old conger-eel, that used to come once a week: **he** taught us Drawling, Stretching and Fainting in Coils.'
> (…)
> 'I never went to him,' the Mock Turtle said with a sigh. 'He taught Laughing and Grief, they used to say.'

Just as the meld pun, **alcoholidays**, contains two words joined together, **alcohol** and **holidays**, there is another form which joins two words into one word, by sacrificing rather than superimposing parts of each word. Such a word is **brunch**, a meal which is a combination of breakfast and lunch, made with **br** from **breakfast** and **unch** from **lunch**. A word like this is called a **portmanteau** word, after Humpty Dumpty's definition in **Through the Looking-Glass**:

> 'Well, "slithy" means "lithe" and "slimy". "Lithe" is the same as "active". You see it's like a portmanteau — there are two meanings packed up into one word.'

The **holorhyme**, or **charade,** is a kind of untangled pun, but it does not pun. One series of letters is given twice, but different words are assembled with them, giving two different meanings:

Q: When is an eye not an eye?

Flamingo: pale, scenting a latent shark!
Flaming, opalescent in gala tents — hark! (Howard Bergerson)

This form is purely visual, it does not work aurally like a true pun. The holorhyme is an extreme form of pun; language has been stretched a long way to concoct these conceits. The relation between the two different meanings of the same set of letters is absolutely distant and arbitrary:

O fly, rich Eros — dogtrot, ski, orbit eras put in swart
Of lyric heros. Dog Trotski or bite Rasputin's wart. (Bergerson)

In contrast to the holorhyme, **homophonic couplets** have been devised* in which the lines, when spoken rapidly, sound interchangeable:

'Let us be true, Tom, let's!' I scream and whine.
Lettuce, beetroot, omelettes, ice-cream and wine. (James Michie)

Conundrum and **riddle** are the names given to the questions which elicit punning or double meaning answers:

Q: What is the difference between the Prince of Wales, an orphan, a bald-headed old man, and a gorilla?
A: The first is an heir apparent, the second has ne'er a parent, the third has no hair apparent, and the fourth has an hairy parent.

It may be that the term conundrum should be applied to questions answered with a pun:

Q: A soldier, sailor and airman got into a car. Which one drove?
A: The soldier because he had the khaki on him.

Similarly, it may be that the term riddle should be applied to questions answered with a play on words:

*cf. **The New Statesman**'s Weekend Competition of 20 August 1976

A: When an onion makes it water.

Q: What stays where it is when it goes off?
A: A gun.

On being shown a plush Manhattan apartment by a real estate agent, Dorothy Parker complained,

> 'Oh, dear, that's much too big. All I need is room enough to lay a hat and a few friends.'

This is another kind of play on words, a play on **lay** meaning 'to set down' and **lay** meaning 'to make love to'. This is called **zeugma**, which means 'yoking'. In a zeugma one verb governs more than one word or phrase, each in a different way. A child wrote:

> On Christmas Day we had goose for dinner and visitors for tea.

The Verb **had** governs both dinner-time goose and tea-time visitors.

A **wellerism**, named after Dickens' character Sam Weller, is a comparison that flies off at a tangent, pivoting around the word **as**:

> 'When you're a married man, Samivel, you'll understand a good many things as you don't understand now; but vether it's worth goin' through so much, to learn so little, as the charity-boy said ven he got to the end of the alphabet, is a matter o' taste.'

The usual meaning of a phrase — often a platitude — is given a new meaning by the clause which follows it at **as**:

> 'I've been struck by the beauty of the place,' as the fresh young man said when the pretty girl slapped him.

The wellerism is a type of the play on words.

The **Tom Swifty**, created by Edward Stratemeyer, is an adverbial pun or play on words:

....

The ground was covered with wooden enemies.

'I'll see if I can dig it up for you,' said Tom gravely.

The adverb **gravely** transforms the meaning of the preceding phrase, from the obvious or normal meaning to another stronger meaning. This example is a play on the word **grave**.

'No, Eve, I won't touch that apple,' said Tom adamantly.

This is an adverbial pun on **adamantly,** reminding us that **Adam** is included within it.

....
Contraception is a sin, as any see can plainly fool.

TWENTY-THREE

Punning Names

When Noel Coward wrote to T.E. Lawrence, who at that time had submerged himself in the persona of Aircraftman Shaw, no. 338171, he began his letter:

Dear 338171 (May I call you 338?).

Names nowadays are largely pure sound. Like Aircraftman Shaw's number they are arbitrarily attached. Surnames used to signify the trade of a person, and Christian names were just that: a person's name meant more than pure sound. Since names today are devoid of meaning and exist only as sound, they present an easy target for the punster.

As a schoolboy Paul Hammond was known as *Hammond Eggs*. Similarly Baden-Powell, the founder of Scouting, was known as *Bathing Towel*. Patrick Hughes tells the story of his father,

Peter Hughes who, glancing up at the licensee's name, Annie Moss, written over the door of her pub, murmured as he entered, 'I hope she doesn't show us any animosity.'

More than one person changed his name from the innocuous **Bates** to something even more innocuous:

An admirer says to President Lincoln, 'Permit me to introduce my family. My wife, Mrs Bates. My daughter, Miss Bates. My son, Master Bates.'
'Oh dear!' replied the President.

....

A gossip is a person with a keen sense of rumour.

Children often make puns on each other's names, as they realise that things, words and sounds are separate entities. This occurs when they learn to read, and see that words can exist visually as well as aurally and orally. A favourite genre of the child-punster is the fictitious book title:

Tripping Over by Lucy Lastick
Cliff Tragedy by Eileen Dover
You Mustn't Climb Trees by Nicholas Lady
Broken Windows by Eva Brick
Rusty Bedsprings by I.P. Freely
I'm Not Scared by Hugo Furst
A Happy Marriage by Maud Fitzgerald and Gerald Fitzmaud
Maths by Adam Upp
Indigestion by Henrietta Bunn.

Perhaps the words in these books are made from the fanciful alphabet that begins:

A for ism
B for mutton
C for yourself ...

The famous are as familiar as our friends. Dorothy Parker said:

That's the trouble with Verlaine — he was always chasing Rimbaud's.

James Joyce wrote of children that

they were jung and easily freudened.

Sometimes people have punning stage names, like Gail Storm who is a film star, and Sandy Shaw who is a pop singer.

....
If all economists were laid end to end, they would not reach a conclusion. (Shaw)

Q. Who invented the steam engine?
A. Watts his name.

This conundrum gives Watt's name and cannot give his name simultaneously. John Donne punned on his own name:

When thou hast done, thou has not done.
For I have more …
And having done that: Thou has done,
   I fear no more.

So did Thomas Hood, who wrote of his own death:

Now the undertaker will earn a livelihood.

(It is easy to miss the pun on **urn** here.)
   Children catch each other out by asking

'How high is a Chinaman?'
'About five foot?'
'No, how high is a Chinaman?'
'Five foot two?'
'No, How Hi is a Chinaman.'

In the following joke an occidental suitor is rebuffed by an oriental rival:

What did Cleopatra say when Mark Anthony asked if she was
true to him?
'Omar Khayyam.'

Cleopatra is saying that she is true to Mark Anthony at the same ti me as she speaks another man's name. Ignorance of a foreign language and a famous film led one reporter to list Bunuel and Dali's **L'Age d'or** as *Large Door* in a London weekly paper. This

....

The inhabitants of the temperate forests earn a living by selling their skins. It is a hard life.

mistake is probably the result of a telephonic misunderstanding, thus reminding us that the pun is about sound. The arbitrary way in which names are assigned to things is pointed up in this reminiscence by Anthea Askey of her famous father, comedian Arthur Askey:

> As a child I never saw a lot of my father. He was away so much, I called him 'Wave'. I thought that was his name because my mother was always saying to me, 'There he goes ... wave!'

Dorothy Parker gave a significant name to her canary, based on one of the bird's habits:

> She called him 'Onan', because he spilled his seed upon the ground.

TWENTY-FOUR

Landscape Puns

Verbal language abounds with anthropomorphic metaphors like 'the brow of the hill', 'the valley of her thighs', 'the eye of the storm', 'the mouth of the cave'. Just as man put himself at the centre of the universe and verbally interpreted the world in his own image — anthropocentrism — so he has made a close visual relation, a type of pun, between nature and his own image.

'Winter' (29), a painting by Joos de Momper (1564–1635), puns on a wintry mountain and an old man's head. From the punster's point of view the landscape as an image provides conveniently malleable material: earth, foliage, water and buildings can take a variety of forms in being adapted to the human physiognomy. (In the 17th century some gardens were constructed in the shape of human bodies, actual puns made of earth and plants.) Such a picture refers by implication to the accidents of vision whereby for a moment a cloud may look like a camel. They epitomise the Renaissance discovery of 'the point of view' and the subsequent emphasis on perspective, which works, theoretically, from only one viewpoint.

....
Q. When is an artist someone to be feared?

29. Joos de Momper, 'Winter', oil painting, c. 1610

....

A. When he draws a gun.

TWENTY-FIVE

Visual Puns on the Face, Breasts, Posterior, and Penis

ON THE FACE

The visual punster knows that just a few clues will lead to the recognition of a face. Alfred Hitchcock's drawing for an (unmade) sequence in one of his early films, **The Lodger** (1926), illustrates this point **(30)**. Hitchcock intended that the scene

30. Alfred Hitchcock, drawing, c. 1966. Courtesy Robert Laffont

One blackbird to another: 'Bred any good rooks lately?'

31. Anon, sculpted skull, c. 6000 B.C.

should show the back of an escaping van. The tops of the heads of the driver and his mate would be seen through the oval windows in the back doors. As the van turned and swerved the occupants' heads, moving from side to side in the windows, would make it look as if the van had a face and was rolling its eyes.

Eyes are the most important element in the configuration of the face. In (31), one of a number of skulls discovered in

....

A carpet is bought by the yard and worn by the foot.

32. Dali parasoaic painting.

....

Booze: the opposite of cheers.

If frozen water is iced water, what is frozen ink?

excavations at Jericho, dating from c. 6000 B.C., cowrie shells are used to represent eyes. The head was made using the skull as an armature, covering it with clay to simulate flesh, and inserting the shells into the eyesockets to become eyes with eyelashes touching.

People often see faces in things. Salvador Dali describes how 'following a period of study — during which I had been completely obsessed — of Picasso's heads, I am looking for an address in a heap of papers when I am struck by a reproduction that I assume to be by Picasso, though it is a completely unknown work. Suddenly the face fades away and I realise it is an illusion.' The photograph in question (32) is of some natives sitting outside a hut. Turn it on its side to see the 'Picasso' head Dali saw. This is a rare instance of actually finding a pun. In Arcimboldo's portrait (33) Calvin's head is made of fish and fowl, his nose is the parson's nose. It says that while Calvin preached asceticism he was a glutton himself.

Arcimboldo imposes his pun on the viewer by a strong use of context and by an accretion of visual detail.

An etching by Martin Van Maele (34) proposes the punning equation nose: penis; jowls: scrotum. His etching is like Magritte's 'The Rape' (20) in that part of the body puns with another part of the body: there is an element of self-reference. Freud suggested that certain parts of the body (eg. the nose) could stand in as erotogenic zones for the genitals, which are thus symbolically displaced upwards. His contemporary Van Maele cheerfully displaces wherever his explicit fancy takes him.

A follower of Arcimboldo painted a portrait of Herod made up of naked children (35). This punning portrait is an allegory: Herod is depicted in the bodies of his victims.

An obvious butt for the punster's wit is Freud (36). As a girl's pubic hair stands for his eyebrow, so by implication a vagina stands for his eye. The picture says that Freud looked at the world through a short-sighted pudendum.

Champagne to your real friends. Real pain to your sham friends!

33. Giuseppe Arcimboldo, 'John Calvin', oil painting, 1566. Courtesy Svenska Portrattarkivet, National-Museum, Stockholm

....

He tried to put my mind at rest but I was using it at the time. (A.F.G. Lewis)

34. Martin Van Maele, engraving from **La Grande Danse Macabre des vifs**, c. 1907

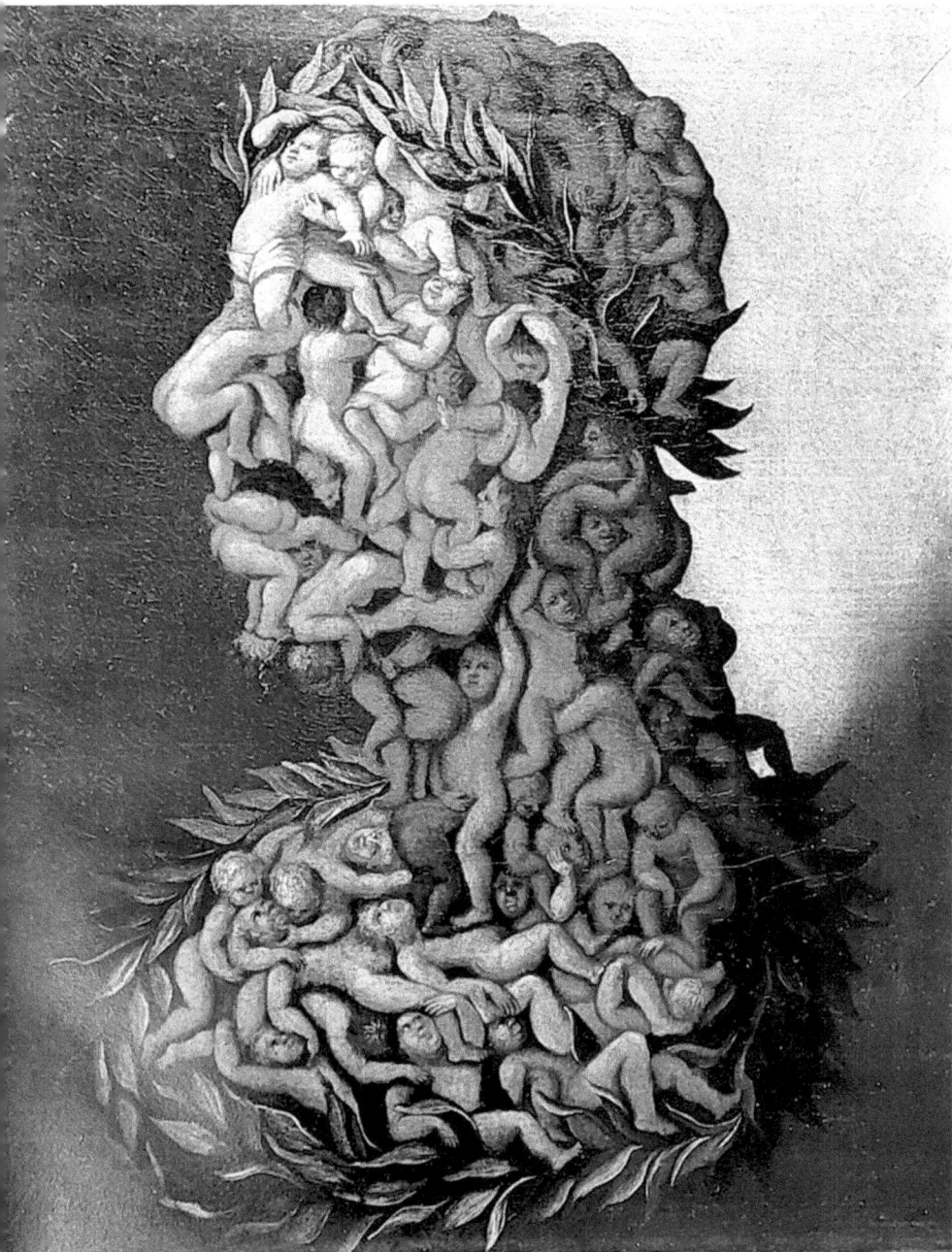

35. Giuseppe Arcimboldo (attrib), 'Herod', oil painting, n.d. Courtesy Galleria d'arte Del Cavallino, Venice

36. Anon, 'Freud', drawing, n.d.

A lover is like a traitor: you can expect to be turned on by either. (A.F.G. Lewis)

ON THE BREASTS

Breasts are easy to represent and are often punned upon. One equation frequently made is between breasts and fruit (37).

37. Anon, 'Who Wants My Apples', photograph, n.d.

....
A drama critic is a man who leaves no turn unstoned. (G.B.Shaw)

Gauguin made a veiled reference to this genre in his 'Tahitiennes au mango' (38).

38. Paul Gauguin, 'Tahitiennes au mango', oil painting, 1899. Metropolitan Museum of Art, New York. Gift of William Church Osborn, 1949

....
They talked together like two egotists/In conversation all made up of eyes. (Thomas Hood)

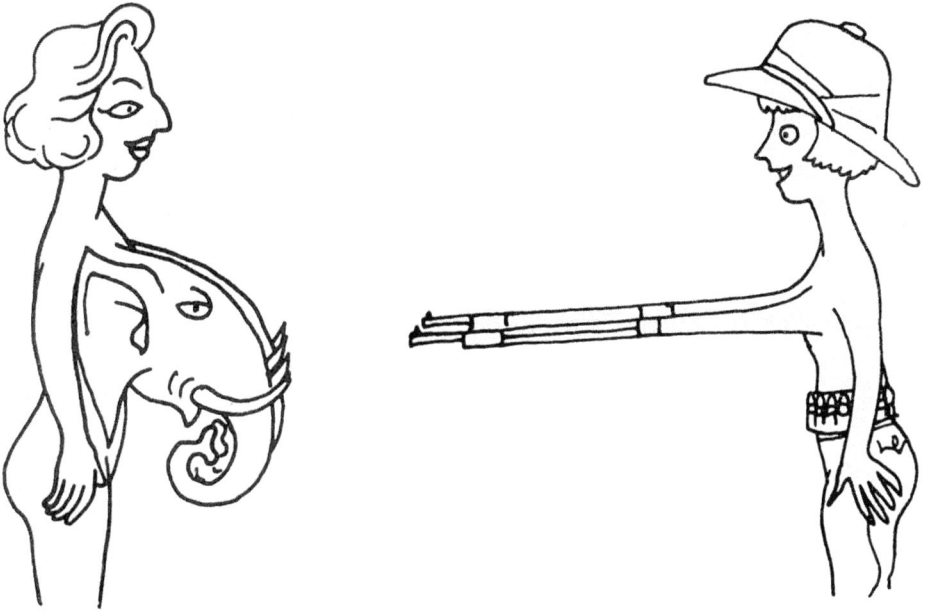

39. Maurice Henry, drawing, n.d. Courtesy J.-J. Pauvert, Paris

While the breast/fruit pun has a particular coherence, there are other puns about breasts that are more far-fetched. Maurice Henry's drawing **(39)** is one such. In his two breast puns the common denominator between breasts and rifles and elephants' heads is merely that they can come in pairs and that they stick out. The context that gives the guns and elephants meaning as breasts is their position on the ladies' chests, and that of big game hunting. The meaning of the cartoon is that we find metaphors for different kinds of breasts.

....

Spooner criticised a student's thesis by saying there were too many prowlers in his hose.

ON THE POSTERIOR

There are no visual puns on elbows. Puns about the body are mostly about the head and the sexual organs. There are some on the buttocks. Donald McGill's postcard (40) is an untangled pun on a baby's head and a baby's backside. (In popular English parlance buttocks are called 'cheeks'.)

A cartoon by Perodin (41) makes an analogy between buttocks and breasts in the form of a pun. A lady at a ball wears a mask of a girl's face on her back and bares her buttocks so that they appear to be breasts.

"So these are your dear twins! And aren't they exactly alike!!"

40. Donald McGill, 'So these are your dear twins! ...', postcard, n.d. Courtesy Basil Buckland

....

What does a mathematician with constipation do?

Perodin

41. Perodin, drawing from Bennett, op.cit., 1953.
Courtesy Simon & Schuster, New York

He works it out with a pencil.

ON THE PENIS

The correlation in spoken language between a cock (bird) and a cock (penis) has existed in visual language for thousands of years. The World's Awakener', an ancient Greek bronze **(42)**, proposes such a relation.

In **Origins**, his etymological dictionary, Eric Partridge, discussing how **cock** came to mean 'penis', says that **cock** , 'male bird', came first to mean **cock**, 'faucet or tap', deriving from a fancied resemblance between a tap and the bird or its head or its comb. He suggests that **cock** later came to mean 'penis' in Standard English in the eighteenth century, deriving from a similarity in shape to a tap and from the fact that both a tap and a penis emit water. Our researches seem to suggest that the relation between **cock**, 'bird', and **cock**, 'penis', is much older than this, and that the tap analogy does not hold water. At the metaphorical level the bird and the penis share qualities of virility, 'of an upright posture when crowing' (Partridge); a beak is fierce, hard and greedy, like an erect penis. The metaphorical cock represents man's idealised view of his own sexual prowess: master of all his hens, the cockerel is up early. In **Metaphor and Reality** (1962) Philip Wheelwright says that a cockerel suggests potency 'which he expresses by crowing in triumph after coition with a hen'. At the purely visual level an analogy is made between the reddish, fleshy wattle and the human scrotum; and the hard, bony beak standing out from the body, and the tumescent cock.

Every schoolboy has heard of 'phallic symbols'. Psychoanalysts believe that the mind hides its libidinous thoughts in symbols, objects in daily life which stand for aspects of sexuality the superego thinks unmentionable. For instance if someone dreams of a chimney, she is dreaming of a penis; if someone dreams of a vase, he is dreaming of a vagina. How do you get a chimney

....

'My mother made me a homosexual.'

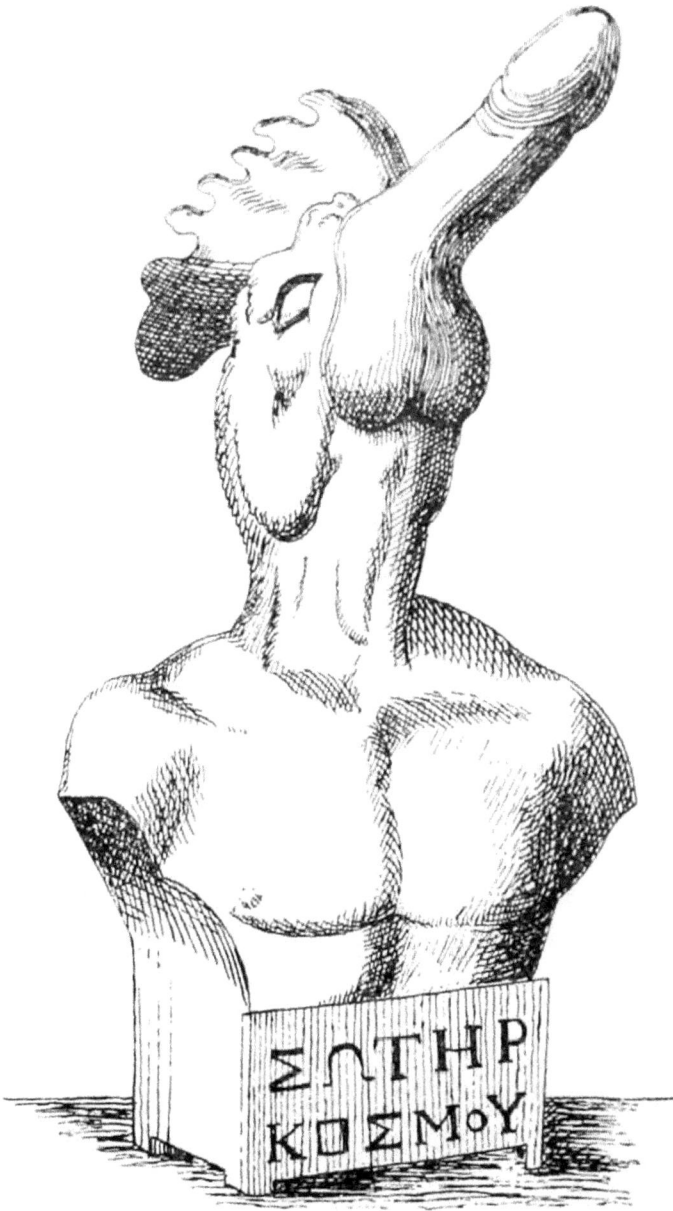

42. Anon, 'The World's Awakener', drawing of an ancient Greek bronze

....

'If I gave her the wool, do you think she'd make me one?'

A Stick of Rock, Cock?

43. Donald McGill, 'A stick of rock, cock?', postcard, c. 1950. Courtesy Basil Buckland

....

Why is painting the hair red like a part of your throat?

into a vase? We ask this only because the erotic puns on the penis operate at a conceptual level, and take no notice of practical matters like the relative size of things.

In his comic postcard **(43)** Donald McGill puns on the penis with a gigantic stick of rock. The man holds the rock as if he is trying to stop this symbolic rock from falling into the symbolic sea.

....

Because it's the carrot dyed art hairy.

44. René Magritte, untitled drawing, n.d.

A further example of the overlap between the visual double entendre and pictorial symbolism is Magritte's drawing **(44)**. In his sophisticated way Magritte has taken the chimney, a phallic symbol **par excellence**, and turned the symbol back into a phallus by the addition of a lady's hand.

....
A couple at a horror film: O how they love each shudder!

TWENTY-SIX

Other Theories of Punnology

While some writers do use the term 'visual pun' (eg. E.H. Gombrich, Rudolf Arnheim, Edmund Carpenter), they do not attempt a definition or theoretical exposition, or a comparison with similar verbal forms. We have tried to show that visual dual meaning has the same rationale as verbal dual meaning.

In the **Oxford English Dictionary** under a heading such as **pun** first a definition of the word is given, then there are appended several examples of the use of the word over the years. Unfortunately some of the definitions of words are misleading, inaccurate, and cursory. Similarly, the examples given of the early and typical use of these words are often inadequate, since they sometimes fail. to give light as to the meaning of the word and merely chronicle a mention.

A **pun** is defined as 'the use of a word in such a way as to suggest two or more meanings or different associations, or the use of two or more words of the same or nearly the same sound with different meanings, so as to produce a humorous effect; a play on words.'

The first part of the definition is too vague. The second part seems to describe what we call the **untangled pun**. The third part of the definition, that the pun is made to produce a humorous effect, is not necessarily true. The fourth part asserts that a pun is a play on words: this is wrong.

Of the nine examples given, two aid definition:

....

The Mexican weather forecast: Chili today and hot tamale.

Addison (1711): 'here define it to be a Conceit arising from the use of two Words that agree in the Sound, but differ in the Sense.' Pope (1727): 'Pun, where a word, like the tongue of a Jackdaw, speaks twice as much by being Split.'

The **play on or upon words** is defined as 'a sportive use of words so as to convey a double meaning, or produce a fantastic or humorous effect by similarity of sound with difference of meaning; a pun.'

The first part of the definition is vague, and misleading — when you see the definition, given below of the **double meaning**. The second part describes a pun more than a play on words. The third part of the definition says that a pun is the same as a play on words: this is wrong.

Of the six examples given, one is interesting:

Robertson (1850): 'It was no mere play of words which induced the apostle to bring these two things (fulness of the Spirit and fulness of wine, Eph. v. 18) together.' This seems to describe a true play on words.

The double entendre is defined as 'a double meaning; a word or phrase having a double sense, esp. as used to convey an indelicate meaning.' Of the five examples given, the most interesting is: Duchess of Cleveland (1678): 'The ambassador showed a letter, which he pretended one part of it was a double entendre.'

The **double meaning** is defined as 'double or ambiguous signification; the use of an ambiguous word or phrase, esp. to convey an indelicate meaning; = double entendre.' Of the six examples given, the most interesting is:

Grote (1853): 'By delicate wit and double-meaning phrases to express an offensive sentiment.'

....

What is worse than raining cats and dogs?

Apart from the first part of the definition of the double meaning, which is very vague indeed, these definitions are the same, and barely adequate.

The **homonym** is defined as '1a — the same name or word used to denote different things' and '1b (philological) — applied to words having the same sound, but differing in meaning: opposite to heteronym and synonym.'

Definition 1a is correct, as far as it goes; definition 1b, the philological meaning, which presumably should be more professional and correct, describes the homophone rather than the homonym.

Two of the three examples are:

Burgersdicius (1697): 'Those (words) that differ not in termination; as **grammatica,** *the art of grammar, and* **grammatica,** *a woman, are not conjugates, but homonyms.'*

Douse (1876): 'A monosyllabic language, indeed, like the Chinese, is but, as it were, a cluster of homonyms.'

The first example does describe homonyms, but presumably of different root meaning, our homonymic pun might be constructed from such material. The second example, implying same-sounding speech, perhaps describes homophony.

The **homophone** is described as '(philological) applied to words having the same sound but differing in meaning or derivation; also to different symbols denoting the same sound or group of sounds'.

The definition of the homophone is quite clear in the first part. It is a little difficult to know what is meant by the second part.

Of the four examples given two are excellent:

F. Hall (1873): 'Homophones, identical to the ear only; as **ail** *and* **ale**.'

....
Hailing taxis.

*I. Taylor (1883): We have in English the four homophones **rite,**
write, right and **wright**. By the aid of the variant spelling
a child readily learns that these homophones are really four
different words.'*

Metathesis is defined as '1a (rhetorical) — the transposition
of words (obsolete)' and '1b (grammatical) — the interchange of
position between sounds or letters in a word; the result of such
a transposition.' The first definition actually seems to describe
chiasmus; the second definition is of a much narrower and less
widely used linguistic form than true metathesis.

The **spoonerism** is defined as 'an accidental transposition
of the initial sounds, or other parts, of two or more words'. No
examples are given. It is ironical that this adequate definition
should be given of the spoonerism, a sub-section of the
metathesis, when no definition is given of the true metathesis.

The **chiasmus** is defined as 'a grammatical figure by which
the order of words in one of two parallel clauses is inverted in the
other.' There is one example, from 1871, which merely names the
word. This definition is adequate, though an example of chiasmus
would help.

Of the minor figures associated with the pun and the play
on words, the **malapropism** is given a fair definition, with
only fair examples; the **howler** is merely defined as 'a glaring
blunder; especially in an examination, etc.', no examples; the
portmanteau word is well defined; the **holorhyme** is not in.
The **conundrum** is given two appropriate definitions: '(3) — a
pun or word-play depending on similarity of sound in words of
different meaning', and a punning example is given: '(4) a riddle
in the form of a question the answer to which involves a pun or
play on words.' We have suggested that the conundrum might
describe the punning question, while the **riddle** might describe
the question which plays on the meaning of words — we had in

....
Q. Why did the farmer give the pig a collar?

mind the way in which the Anglo-Saxon Riddles turned upon different meanings of the same words and phrases. The pertinent OED definition of riddle is 'a question or statement intentionally worded in a dark or puzzling manner, and propounded in order that it may be guessed or answered, especially as a form of pastime; an enigma; a dark saying.' **Zeugma** is accurately defined, the **Wellerism** is poorly defined with poor examples, the **Tom Swifty**, **contrepèterie**, and **adianoeta** are not in.

Sometimes, because of the poverty or inadequacy of the definition in **The Oxford English Dictionary**, the abridged definition given in **The Shorter Oxford English Dictionary**, which consists of 2,672 pages, is disgraceful. Here the **play on words** is very well hidden in the definition of 'play' and is given in one word — 'pun'!

The relevant article in *The Encyclopedia Britannica is* entitled **Figures of Speech**, and is to be found in Volume 9, pp. 257–260. It is written by Marjorie Boulton, Principal of the Charlotte Mason College, Ambleside, England. (Amongst other works, Ms Boulton is the author of **Zamenof, Creator of Esperanto**). Marjorie Boulton confuses the pun with the play on words, she does not understand the double entendre, only takes metathesis as the transposition of letters within a word, includes the spoonerism but not the chiasmus. The homonym and homophone are not discussed anywhere in this edition. Boulton's bibliography lacks a good deal, Lanham (1969) for instance.

The study of the pun, the play on words, double entendre, chiasmus and metathesis is a branch of rhetoric. The Greeks and Romans had comprehensive rules of rhetoric. An excellent modern dictionary of these forms is Richard A. Lanham's **A Handlist of Rhetorical Terms** (1968). Lanham lists all the known terms of rhetoric, giving their Greek, Latin, Shakespearian and modern English names. He briefly and concisely describes the forms. Lanham thus defines the pun, the double entendre,

....

A. To go with his pigsty.

chiasmus, metathesis and malapropism, giving examples of each. Unfortunately he does not understand the play on words, although he does describe several related refinements. Furthermore his definition of metathesis misses the point.

Sigmund Freud, in his **Jokes and Their Relation to the Unconscious** (1905), devotes some seventy-four pages to a chapter entitled 'The Technique of Jokes'. This chapter contains twenty definitions of different kinds of verbal dual meaning under seven heads. Freud ignores rhetorical knowledge and its system of classification. He prefers to analyse the technique of joking in a novel, intuitive way. This individualistic way of thinking leads to a rather confused model. Some of the sub-divisions Freud makes are very slight. While not necessarily naming the forms according to custom Freud does discuss the pun, the meld pun, the untangled pun, the play on words, the double entendre, chiasmus. He does not describe the spoonerism or metathesis. Freud's study of verbal dual meaning is idiosyncratic system-building, the psychoanalysis comes later in the book.

For clarity's sake the definitions of homophone and homonym should be mutually exclusive. While homonyms do sound the same it is silly to call them homophones. Robert Bridges, in his forty-five-page essay 'On English Homophones' (1919), says 'When two or more words different in origin and signification are pronounced alike, whether they are alike or not in their spelling, they are said to be homophonous, or homophones of each other. Such words if spoken without context are of ambiguous signification. Homophone is strictly a relative term, but it is convenient to use it absolutely, and to call any word of this kind a homophone.' This definition is confusing. Words having the same spelling and different meaning — homonyms — have **usually** diverged in meaning from a common original meaning. Words having different spelling and a similar sound — homophones — have **usually** no relation in meaning, this is

....

What has four legs and flies?

just an accident of language. In his zeal to attack the ambiguity inherent in homophones and homonyms, Bridges confuses the two. His bizarre thesis is that the teaching of the South English dialect in the Public Schools, guided by phonetic theories of elocution, tended to produce a pronunciation which gives rise to homophones (he says it is a kind of lazy speech). Bridges gives a list of 'homophones', which includes both homophones and homonyms, totalling 1,775 words. It begins 'arc, ark. arm (**limb**), arm (**weapon**). alms, arms.' Bridges claims that an average educated man's vocabulary numbers between 3,000 and 5,000 words, and that 1,600 to 2,000 words are homophonous: amazingly, he suggests that a third of the words we use are therefore confusing. Bridges briefly considers the pun and the play on words, and their need of homophones and homonyms (he denies that the loss of homophones would lead to the loss of the pun, claiming that more tortured homophony would be attempted). Bridges ignores the role of context in conveying the meaning of ambiguous words; for instance if we say 'he threw the ball in an arc' we do not imagine it hit Noah on the head.

In his book **Which Witch?** (1966) Julian Franklyn takes up where Bridges left off. The main body of this book is a 198-page dictionary of homophones and homonyms. It begins 'A, Aye, Aye, Eh, Eye, I'. He often writes a few lines incorporating the homophones and homonyms: 'Eh? What's that? You don't wish to come for a walk with me? I do not investigate your reason from A to Z — but I have my eye on it: a promise of ice-cream will induce you to change your "no" to "aye", eh? or will you sulk for aye?' The dictionary is preceded by an essay entitled 'Sight, Sense and Sound', which is about similarities in appearance, meaning and pronunciation of certain English words. Franklyn compounds the errors of Bridges with regard to homophones and homonyms. He appeals to the **Oxford English Dictionary**, saying 'and higher authority there is none', for some extremely

....
A dead horse.

ambiguous and unhelpful definitions. Franklyn is misled by that dictionary's inability to distinguish clearly between homophone and homonym: he should have examined their roots. He even introduces a new word into the discussion, **homograph**, meaning 'a word of the same spelling as another, but of different origin and meaning': this is either our homonymic pun, or a word like **lead**, which can be a heavy metal or mean 'to go first, act as a guide', depending on its pronunciation. Franklyn says 'homonyms are inherently humorous', and he prizes the pun. As the author of a book called **The Cockney** he does not take Bridges' attack on Southern English very seriously, but takes pronunciation and homophony rather as they come.

The Reverend Walter W. Skeat's **An Etymological Dictionary of the English Language** (1882) gives a list of homonyms'. He prefaces his list, '**Homonyms** are words spelt alike, but differing in use. In a few cases, I include different uses of what is either exactly, or nearly, the word, at the same time noting that the forms are allied; but in most.cases, the words are of different origin.' That is, Skeat is saying that most of his examples are our homonymic puns. In fact, most of the words in Skeat's list are of the same etymological origin, though some are not. His list begins 'Abide (1), to wait for. (E.); Abide (2), to suffer for a thing. (E.); Allow (1), to assign, grant. (F., -L.); Allow (2), to approve of. (F., -L.); An (1), the indef. article. (E.); An (2), if. (Scand.)'. He firstly gives 1,250 words, each of which is then paired, sometimes tripled.

Willard R. Espy, in **The Game of Words** (1971), gives a list called a 'homonym lexicon', which is a list of homophones. Espy's list of homonyms does not contain one homonym. It begins 'Acclamation, acclimation; Ad, add; Adds, ads, adze'. It contains approximately 500 words, each with one or two homophones, perhaps 1,200 words altogether. (One way for the devoted searcher to find homophones is to look in a rhyming dictionary.)

....

Why is the Prince of Wales, musing on his mother's government, like a rainbow?

John Orr's **Three Studies on Homonymics** (1962) is the work of a professor of linguistics. In a Socratic dialogue he discusses minutely a special dynamic of the development of the French language. His argument is that when two similar sounding words are within the same psychological orbit (or range of meaning) one word may take over some of the functions of its phonetic neighbour. In the course of this erudite discussion of etymology he has some interesting things to say about punning: 'Pity the poor punster! He has his place in the linguistic scheme like his more respectable colleague the rhymer. They are merely extremists — particularly the rhymer! — playing tricks, each of them, with the normal use of speech, playing with words, as we say, and all do, more or less. Only, the punster does it for the pure fun of the thing; he is an artist, and his motto **'l'art pour 'l'art'**. The punster startles us by bringing into the same psychological field — I hope you'll accept that — sounds and ideas which in the practice of our speech are far apart. The punster would have no **locus standi** were it not for the tendency of our words to become arbitrary, non-motivated linguistic signs.' Orr's view of language is opposite to Bridges'. He notices that homophones and other accidents are part of the life of language; only an artificial language, he remarks, would be without them.

Clifton Fadiman's book **Appreciations** (1962) contains the essay 'Small Excellencies: A Dissertation on Puns'. Fadiman is a **littérateur** with a love of puns. He includes twenty-nine different types of pun, which include plays on words, malapropisms, chiasmi and spoonerisms. His formal distinctions are sometimes petty-minded, and he misses the important distinctions. For example, he lists as different types of pun sentences having two puns, he calls this the 'double pun', and sentences having three puns, he calls these the 'triple pun'. On the other hand he does not describe the essential difference between the pun and the

....

Because it's the son's reflection on a steady reign.

play on words. As a critical model Fadiman's system is not up to much; as a picturesque exercise in punnology it has charm.

Another literary gent, Bevis Hillier, has entertained us with an essay on the pun in his Introduction to **Punorama** (1974), a selection of the Victorian puns of the Hon. Hugh Rowley. Hillier begins his Introduction with many quotations from eminent writers for and against the pun, before presenting his model, consisting of ten main types. His theorising is always entertaining, often inaccurate, not very methodical, and biased towards Eng. Lit.

Both Fadiman and Hillier do not go far enough. They do not consider etymology, homophony or homonymy; they do not consider chiasmus and metathesis properly. Peter Farb says in **Word Play** (1974) 'the obscene pun is a major variety of the form'. Hillier and Fadiman are girlish when faced with rudeness.

We have read one book and three papers on spoonerisms, slips of the tongue and metathesis. William Hayter's **Spooner, A Biography** (1977) is the first biography of the man Spooner and rather a full dish. Hayter uses the term 'metaphasis' (which is not in the **OED**) rather than metathesis in his ten-page chapter on spoonerisms. In 'The Warden's Wordplay: Toward a Redefinition of the Spoonerism' (1966) Rossell Hope Robbins is critical of the attributions of almost all spoonerisms to Spooner: he claims only three spoonerisms were authentic. He includes, as part of his text, an anthology of ten chiasmi and almost sixty metatheses and spoonerisms.

A thorough study of slips of the tongue, touching on metathesis, the malapropism and the spoonerism is Charles F. Hockett's paper 'Where the Tongue Slips, There Slip I' (1967). Hockett is a linguist and a renegade Chomskyite. He considers verbal mistakes as clues to the way we form normal speech. He includes and analyses many mundane conversational slips.

....

A raven is like a writing-desk because it bodes ill for owed bills. (James Michie)

Hockett's pedantry is sometimes superficial: he thinks the double entendre is the play on words, and he does not think there is any point in making the distinction between a double entendre (by which he means the play on words) and a pun.

Another modern linguist who has studied errors of speech is Victoria A. Fromkin in her 'Slips of the Tongue' (1973). Like Hockett, Fromkin believes that slips of the tongue reveal the basic structures of language. She analyses the various forms such errors may take, including the spoonerism.

Following on from 'Upon the Pun' (1978) Walter Redfern's 'Puns' (1984) and John Pollack's 'The Pun Also Rises' (2011) are both excellent. Redfern and Pollack accept our analyses of verbal wordplay, but they do not consider visual puns and so on. On the other hand, the empty 'On Puns – The Foundation of Letters' (1988), edited by Jonathan Culler, is an exemplary example of ignorant academic gobbledygook.

....

'I'll be with you in necks to no time,' said the executioner. (A.F.G. Lewis)

(ed.) James A.H. Murray, Henry Bradley, W.A. Craigie, C.T. Onions, **The Oxford English Dictionary**, Oxford University Press, Oxford, 1933 (reprinted 1961).

(ed.) R.W. Burchfield, **A Supplement to the Oxford English Dictionary, Volume I, A-G**, Oxford University Press, Oxford, 1972.

(ed.) R.W. Burchfield, **A Supplement to the Oxford English Dictionary, Volume II, H-N**, Oxford University Press, Oxford, 1976.

(ed.) Warren E. Preece, **The Encyclopedia Britannica**, Encyclopedia Britannica, Inc., Chicago, 1973.

Richard A. Lanham, **A Handlist of Rhetorical Terms**, University of California Press, Berkeley, 1969.

Sigmund Freud, **Jokes, and their Relation to the Unconscious**, Routledge and Kegan Paul, London, 1966.

Robert Bridges, 'On English Homophones', in **The Society For Pure English Tract No. II**, Oxford, 1919.

Julian Franklyn, **Which Witch? Being a Grouping of Phonetically Compatible Words**, Hamish Hamilton, London, 1966.

Reverend Walter W. Skeat, M.A., **An Etymological Dictionary of the English Language**, Clarendon Press, Oxford, 1882.

Willard R. Espy, **The Game of Words**, Wolfe Publishing Company, London, 1971.

John Orr, **Three Studies on Homonymics**, Edinburgh University Press, 1962.

Clifton Fadiman, 'Small Excellencies: A Dissertation on Puns', in **Appreciations**, Hodder & Stoughton, London, 1962.

Bevis Hillier & Peter MacKarell, **Punorama, or The Best of the Worst**, Whittington Press, Andoversford, 1974.

William Hayter, **Spooner, A Biography**, W.H. Allen, London, 1977.

Włodzimierz Sobkowiak, **Metaphonology of English Parono-masic Puns**, Verlag Peter Lang GmbH, Frankfurt am Main, 1991.

Edward Le Comte, **A Dictionary of Puns in Milton's English Poetry**, Columbia University Press, New York, 1981.

James B. Hobbs, **Homophones and Homographs, An American Dictionary, Third Ed.**, McFarland & Company, Inc., 1999.

Nils W. Lund, **Chiasmus in the New Testament, A Study in the Form and Function of Chiastic Structures**, University of North Carolina Press, Chapel Hill, NC, 1942 (reprinted 1970 and 1992).

John W. Welch, **Chiasmus in Antiquity**, Research Press Reprint Edition, Provo, Utah, 1999.

Wolfgang Mieder and Stewart A. Kingsbury, **A Dictionary of Wellerisms**, Oxford University Press, 1984

Michael West, **Transcendental Wordplay**, Ohio University Press, Athens, 2000.

Rossell Hope Robbins, 'The Warden's Wordplay: Towards a Redefinition of the Spoonerism', in **The Dalhousie Review**, Halifax, Nova Scotia, Winter 1966–67.

Charles F. Hockett, Where the Tongue Slips, There Slip I', in **To Honor Roman Jakobson**, vol. II, Mouton, The Hague, 1967.

Victoria A. Fromkin, 'Slips of the Tongue', in **Scientific American**, December 1973.

Bibliographies

1. VERBAL MATERIAL

A. Secondary Theories of Punnology

Peter Farb, **Word Play**, Jonathan Cape, London, 1974.
A popularised account of what the modern linguist knows and thinks. He mentions the erotic pun in his wise discussion of 'the speakable and the unspeakable'. The book's title is rather misleading.

(ed) J.T. Shipley, **A Dictionary of World Literary Terms**, George Allen and Unwin, London, 1970.
In his article on the pun Shipley mentions nine types. These categories are usually weak or wrong.

J.A. Cuddon, **A Dictionary of Literary Terms**, Andre Deutsch, London, 1977.
This author is correct on the homophone, nearly correct on the homonym, average on the spoonerism, poor on the pun and the chiasmus. He has nothing on the play on words, calls the double entendre un mot a double entente, and has a very narrow definition of the metathesis.

Eugene S. McCartney, 'Puns and Plays on Proper Names', in **The Classical Journal** 19, 1919.
Discusses puns in Latin and Greek; 330 puns and word plays quoted or listed. 'The Romans loved the clashing of word on word as well as of sword on sword. They were fond of plays which depended for their effect upon similarity or identity of sound at the beginning, middle, or end of words, whether they were etymologically related or not.'

C.J. Fordyce, 'Puns on Names in Greek', in **The Classical Journal** 28, 1932–33.
Note to McCartney. Adds a few Greek examples.

M.M. Mahood, **Shakespeare's Wordplay**, Methuen, London, 1957.
A very full study of the puns etc. in Shakespeare.

Dr. F.A. Bather, 'The Puns of Shakespeare', in (ed) Rev. C. Halford Hawkins, **Noctes Shaksperianae**, Castle and Lamb, London, 1887.
Although he is not quite sure what a pun is, Bather has counted all the puns in Shakespeare: there are 1,062. His table of plays arranged in decreasing order of puns per 100 lines matches very closely the accepted chronology of the 37 plays. Individual and inquisitive.

Eric Partridge, **Shakespeare's Bawdy**, Routledge and Kegan Paul, London, 1968.
A fine book of metaphors, symbolism, double entendre and sometimes puns. 'Country matters' (**Hamlet**) is a lewd pun.

Jonathan Swift, 'A Modest Defence of Punning; or a compleat Answer to a scandalous and malicious Paper called God's Revenge Against Punning', Cambridge, 1716, in **Collected Writings**, vol. IV, Basil Blackwell, Oxford, 1957.
'That Gentleman (whoever he was) who lately under the Name of **J. Baker Knight**, thought fit to publish a Discourse entitled God's Revenge against Punning seems to have **founded** his whole Discourse upon one grand Mistake: And therefore his whole Discourse will be **founddead** as soon as I have removed that Mistake; which is, that He condemns the whole Art in general without distinguishing Puns into Good and Bad, whereby it appears how ignorant he is in Antiquity.'

Tom Pun-Sibi (Jonathan Swift), **The Art of Punning; Or, The Flower of Languages; In Seventy-Nine Rules: For the Farther Improvement of Conversation and Help of Memory**, J. Roberts, London, 1719.
'Puns are like so many **Torch-Lights** in the Head, that give the **Soul** a very **distinct View** of those **Images**, which she before seem'd to groap after, as if she had been imprison'd in a Dungeon.'

William Empson, **Seven Types of Ambiguity**, 3rd edition, Pelican Books, Harmondsworth, 1973.
Uses the word 'pun' in a very wide sense. Empson's third type of ambiguity seems to be the pun.

Howard W. Bergerson, **Palindromes and Anagrams**, Dover Publications, New York, 1973.
Has a chapter on 'Palindromes and Charades', with many brilliant examples of the holorhyme, which the author calls the charade.

Luc Etienne, **L'Art du contrepet**, J.-J. Pauvert, Paris, 1971.
Classic study of the **contrepèterie**, with a history of the genre, classifications and technical guidance for the do-it-yourselfer.

John M. Allegro, **The Sacred Mushroom and the Cross**, revised edition, Abacus, London, 1973.
Idiosyncratic study of early Christian cults and iconography. He finds visual and verbal puns on the penis, an hallucinatory mushroom and the Christian Cross. Speculative etymology.

Francis Huxley, **The Raven and the Writing Desk**, Thames and Hudson, London, 1976.
An examination of Carroll's nonsense which is nonsense itself. Much punning and far-fetched etymology.

Charles Jencks & Nathan Silver, **Adhocism**, Secker & Warburg, London, 1972.
Architects consider using things in new improvised ways. This is sometimes a kind of visual punning.

Noah Jonathan Jacobs, **Naming-Day in Eden**, revised edition, Macmillan, New York, 1969.
A study of the various theories of the origin of language presented in the form of scenes in the Garden of Eden. Very funny and learned, even though he never mentions sex!

R.D. Laing, **The Divided Self**, Pelican, Harmondsworth, 1975.
A study of schizophrenia. Schizophrenics often make puns and other word plays: Julie, one of Laing's patients, said she 'was a "tolled bell" (or "told belle"). In other words, she was only what she was told to do.' (cf. Hood's 'the sexton toll'd the bell', and Vinson's For whom the belle toils'.)

Charles Lamb, 'Popular Fallacies: IX. That the Worst Puns Are the Best', in **The Essays of Elia and The Last Essays of Elia**, Oxford University Press, London, 1969.
Joseph Addison, 'The Spectator, no. 61 (Thursday, May 10, 1711)', in Addison, Steele, and others, **The Spectator**, vol. 1, Everyman Library, London, 1970.

b) Collections of Verbal Puns

Phineas Fletcher, **The Purple Island**, Burton & Briggs, London, 1816.
An extended allegory in verse on the human body as an island, first published in 1633. Here he is referring to the teeth:

> *At that cave's mouth, twice sixteen porters stand,*
> *Receivers of the customary rent.*

Hon. Hugh Rowley, **Gamosagammon; or, Hints on Hymen**, John Camden Hotten, London, n.d.
Hon. Hugh Rowley, **Puniana**, Chatto & Windus, London, 1867.
Hon. Hugh Rowley, **Sage Stuffing For Green Goslings**, George Routledge & Sons, London, 1872.

Hon. Hugh Rowley, **More Puniana**, Chatto & Windus, London, 1875.

Rowley is the typical, relentless, Victorian punster. Each of his books is packed with puns, metatheses, and chiasmi. He also drew amusing decorative capitals for his books, a kind of visual pun to accompany his verbal punning:

> *What is tantalizing?*
> *Giving invitations only to teas.*

(ed) Allan Hall, **Worse Verse From Look!**, Times Newspapers Ltd., London, n.d.

(ed) Allan Hall, **More Worse Verse From Look!**, Times Newspapers Ltd., London, 1972.

Two anthologies of punning poems published in the London **Sunday Times**:

> *When does calf love*
> *Become foot fetichism? (Roland Faulkner).*

A.F.G. Lewis, **Weakly Through 1973 With AFGL**, High Wycombe, 1972.

A.F.G. Lewis, **Weakly Through 1974 With AFGL**, High Wycombe, 1973.

A.F.G. Lewis, **Weakly Through 1975 With AFGL**, High Wycombe, 1974.

A.F.G. Lewis, **Weakly Through 1976 With AFGL**, High Wycombe, 1975.

A.F.G. Lewis, **A Pun My Soul**, High Wycombe, 1977.

A.F.G. Lewis is the best and most prolific of the punsters who contribute verse to the newspaper above. These four calendars have a punning verse by him for each week of the year:

> *Do flagellants find*
> *That the switch*
> *Turns them on?*

Bennett Cerf, **Bennett Cerf's Treasury of Atrocious Puns**, Harper & Row, New York, 1968.

They really are atrocious, unoriginal, bowdlerised:

Q. What's a crick?

A. The noise made by a Japanese camera.

Simon Phillips, **The World's Worst Puns**, Wolfe Publishing Company, London, 1969.

One of a series of modern chap books from this publisher. More quantity, than quality, in a dictionary format:

Ping Pong: The smell of a ping.

John S. Crosbie, **Crosbie's Dictionary of Puns**, Pocket Books, Ontario, 1972.

The largest of the pun dictionaries. Shows a natural bias towards North American pronunciation and local references:

Male: A miss is as good as a male. (Old Greek Proverb).

Norman Hunter, **Professor Branestawm's Dictionary**, Puffin Books, Harmondsworth, 1974.

A slim volume intended for children. Mostly single words given a new meaning:

Sediment: What he announced he had in mind.

Afferbeck Lauder (pseud. Alistair Morrison), **Let Stalk Strine**, Wolfe Publishing Company, London.

Afferbeck Lauder, **Nose Tone Unturned**, Wolfe Publishing Company, London.

Afferbeck Lauder, **Fraffly Well Spoken**, Wolfe Publishing Company, London, 1968.

Morrison's books describe the eccentric pronunciation of English by Australians and the upper classes. At his best he gives a word which means something quite different when one knows the phonetic system he is parodying:

Gloria Soame: Australian for 'Glorious Home'.
Bessa Clare: Upper class for 'basically'.

G. Legman, **The Limerick**, Jupiter Books, London, 1974.
Originally published in 1964, this is the best and most complete collection of limericks, 1,739 examples, non-bowdlerised. The limerick often includes a pun or double entendre:

A notorious whore named Miss Hearst
In the weakness of men is well versed.
Reads a sign o'er the head
Of her well-rumpled bed:
'The customer always comes first.'

G. Legman, **Rationale of the Dirty Joke**, Jonathan Cape, London, 1969.
A **tour de force**. Legman is a great scholar in a strange field. This massive tome is packed with rude jokes involving word play. Legman himself does not approve of the pun, he calls it the 'mere pun':

Wedding toast of the latest bride of a much-married playboy:
'It's been hard for some of the others, but it's pretty soft for me.'

G. Legman, **Rationale of the Dirty Joke. Second Series**, Breaking Point Inc., New York, 1975.
Equally delightful polemic, but with far less word play.
Iona & Peter Opie, **The Lore and Language of Schoolchildren**, Oxford University Press, London 1967.
The Opies consider children's speech, which is full of puns. Chapter 5, 'Riddles', contains many:

Q: What is black and white and red all over?
A: A newspaper.

Frank Muir & Dennis Norden, **You Can't Have your Kayak and Heat It**, Eyre Methuen, London, 1973.

Frank Muir & Denis Norden, **Upon My Word**, Eyre Methuen, London, 1974.

Two collections of anecdotes from a radio panel game called 'My Word'. Each comedian is given in turn a well-known phrase or saying. He then tries to construct an even more elaborate shaggy dog story than his opponent, which ends in a pun on the given phrase:

> *In the great right of an excessive wrong (Browning)*

becomes

> *In the grate, right off an excessive rung (Norden).*

Raymond Roussel, 'How I Wrote Certain Of My Books', translated by Trevor Winkfield, Sun Publications, New York, 1975.

Roussel is the Muir and Norden of Literature. In his posthumous work **Comment j'ai écrit certains de mes livres** (1935) Roussel describes a method of writing similar to that of the 'My Word' team: 'In the case of **billard** and **pillard** the two phrases I obtained were:

> *1. Les lettres du blanc sur les bandes du vieux billard ...*
> *(The white letters on the cushions of the old billiard table ...)*
> *2. Les lettres du blanc sur les bandes du vieux pillard ...*
> *(The white man's letters on the hordes of the old plunderer ...)'*

The artist, Marcel Duchamp was influenced by Roussel, and constructed many puns himself, cf.

Marcel Duchamp, **Salt Seller**, Oxford University Press, New York, 1975.

Michel Sanouillet, 'Marcel Duchamp and the French Intellectual Tradition', in Anne d'Harnoncourt & Kingston McShine, **Marcel Duchamp**, Thames & Hudson, London, 1974.

Thomas Hood, **Whimsicalities and Warnings**, Panther Books, London, 1970.

An available edition of the great Victorian punning poet. Hood's black humour, populism and word play make an agreeable whole:

> *His death, which happened in his berth,*
> *At forty-odd befell:*
> *They went and told the sexton, and*
> *The sexton toll'd the bell. ('Faithless Sally Brown', 1826).*

c) Further Verbal Bibliography

Lewis Carroll, 'Letter to Miss Henrietta & Master Edwin Dodgson', in **The Works of Lewis Carroll**, Spring Books, London, 1965.

(ed) Martin Gardner, **The Annotated Alice**, Penguin Books, Harmondsworth, 1965.

Robert D. Sutherland, **Language and Lewis Carroll**, Mouton, The Hague, 1970.

William T. Dobson, **Literary Frivolities, Fancies, Follies and Frolics**, Chatto & Windus, London, 1880.

William T. Dobson, **Poetical Ingenuities and Eccentricities**, Chatto & Windus, London, 1882.

Anthony Burgess, **Joysprick. An introduction to the Language of James Joyce**, Andre Deutsch, London, 1973.

Dmitri A. Borgmann, **Language on Vacation**, Charles Schribner's Sons, New York, 1965.

Dmitri A. Borgmann, **Beyond Language**, Charles Scribner's Sons, New York, 1967.

Gary Jennings, **Personalities of Language**, Victor Gollancz, London 1967.

James Lipton, **An Exaltation of Larks or, The 'Venereal' Game**, Angus & Robertson, London, 1970.

Luis d'Antin Van Rooten, **Mots d'Heures: Gousses, Rames**, Angus & Robertson, London, 1968.

Norman Douglas, **Some Limericks**, Grove Press, New York, 1967.

W.S. Baring-Gould, **The Lure of the Limerick**, Panther, London, 1970.

(ed) Joseph Weintraub, **The Wit and Wisdom of Mae West**, G.P. Putnam's Sons, New York, 1967.

Ennis Rees, **Pun Fun**, Abelard-Schuman, London, 1965.

Louis A. Safian, **Just For the Pun of It**, Abelard-Schuman, London, 1966.

Ben Trovato, **Best Howlers**, Wolfe Publishing Company, London, 1970.

Tom Storey & Sean Gilroy, **The World's Worst Jokes**, Wolfe Publishing Company, London, 1968.

Brams, **Best Schoolboy Jokes**, Wolfe Publishing Company, London, 1969.

John Burn Bailey, **The World's Worst Riddles**, Wolfe Publishing Company, London, 1968.

Arthur Koestler, **The Act of Creation**, revised edition, Pan Books, London, 1970.

Edmund Carpenter & Ken Heyman, **They Became What They Beheld**, Outerbridge & Dienstrey, New York, 1970.

Sigmund Freud, **The Psychopathology of Everyday Life**, Ernest Benn, London, 1966.

Martha Wolfenstein, **Children's Humor. A Psychological Analysis**, The Free Press, Glencoe, Illinois, 1954.

2. VISUAL MATERIAL

a) Visual Puns, Double Meaning and the Double Entendre

Edouard Fuchs, **L'Element erotique dans la caricature**, C.W. Stern, Vienna, 1906.

A massive work of scholarship containing many erotic puns from the art of all periods, much of which is still unknown to a wide audience. Fuchs compiled several similar books, e.g. **Geschichte der erotischen Kunst**(1912).

Jean Boullet, **Symbolisme sexuel, J.-J.** Pauvert, Paris, 1961.
A complementary book to Fuchs on a more popular level, containing many illustrations. Visual symbolism and punning are equated.

Salvador Dali, **Les Metamorphoses erotiques,** Edita, Lausanne, 1969.
Erotic visual puns made by drawing on an illustrated school primer. A rare and barely-known work of the Thomas Hood of fine art. Facsimilies of the original source material are included for comparison.

Graham Lethbridge & John Clarke, **Peek-a-Boob,** Jupiter Books, London, 1974.
Bad taste writ large. Visual and verbal jokes on the female breast, literally.

Annette Messager Truqueuse, **La Femme et ...,** Ecart Publications, Geneva, 1975.
Arty book by an artist who draws pictures on her own body.

Robert Williams Wood, **How To Tell The Birds From The Flowers,** Dover Publications, New York, 1959.
Untangled visual puns, accompanied by humorous rhymes, originally published in 1917. These drawings, by an American physicist, are unique, resourceful, and unscientific.

Benno Geiger, **I Dipinti Ghiribizzosi di Giuseppe Arcimboldi,** Valecchi Editore, Florence, 1954.
The first full-length study of the great visual punster. Some of Geiger's attributions are suspect. The mechanics of visual punning are not considered.

F.-C. Legrand & Felix Sluys, **Arcimboldo et les arcimboldesques**, editions d'Art Andre de Rache, Aalter, 1955.
As academic as Geiger's book, though the attributions are less suspect. Includes related works from other periods and cultures.

Paul Arthur, 'Henry Rox', in **Graphis**, Zurich, Jan-Feb. 1956.
An illustrated article about a modern graphic designer working in the Arcimboldo manner. An excellent introduction to his work are his illustrations to James Laver, **Tommy Apple**, Jonathan Cape, London, 1935.

b) Visual Chiasmus & Metathesis

Peter Newell, **Topsys and Turvys**, Dover Publications, New York, 1964.
A selection from two books first published in 1893 and 1894. A picture on each page is reversible, with an explanatory legend. Drawings of a strange symmetry and elastic style.

Gustave Verbeek, **The Incredible Upside-Downs**, The Rajah Press, New Jersey, 1963.
Originally published as a comic strip in a New York newspaper in 1903–5. Read each page, turn it upside-down and read it again.

Laurence & Rex Whistler, **Oho!**, The Bodley Head, London, 1946.
A collection of invertible heads, of English types, by artist Rex. Brother Laurence wrote the words.

c) Further Visual Bibliography

Paul Wescher, 'The Idea in Giuseppe Arcimboldo's Art', in **The Magazine of Art**, New York, Jan. 1950.
Bernard Denvir, 'Arcimboldo', in (ed) John Hadfield, **The Saturday Book 24**, Hutchinson, London, 1964.
Alfred H. Barr, **Fantastic Art, Dada, Surrealism**, Museum of Modern Art, New York, 1936.

Jurgis Baltrusaitis, '18th Century Gardens and Fanciful Landscapes', in **The Magazine of Art, New** York, April 1952.

..., **Out of this World; An Exhibition of Fantastic Landscapes From the Renaissance to the Present,** University of St. Thomas, Texas, 1964.

(ed) Gert Schiff, **The Amorous Illustrations of Thomas Rowlandson,** Cythera Press, New York, 1969.

Laure Garcin, J.-J. **Grandville,** Eric Losfeld, Paris, 1970.

(ed) Mel L. Sokolow, **The Satyrical Drawings of Martin van Maele,** Cythera Press, New York, 1970.

(ed) Edna Bennett, **The Best Cartoons From France,** Simon & Schuster, New York, 1953.

(ed) Jacques Sternberg & Michel Caen, **Les Chefs-d'œuvre du dessin d'humour,** éditions Planète, Paris, 1968.

Tomi Lingerer, **Horrible,** Hamish Hamilton, London, 1960.

Wieland Herzfelde, **John Heartfield. Leben and Werk,** Der Verlag der Kunst, Dresden, 1962.

Konrad Farner & Heiri Strub, **John Heartfield, Krieg im Frieden,** Hanser Verlag, Munich, 1972.

Salvador Dali, 'Communication: visage paranoiaque', in **Le Surréalisme au service de la Révolution,** no 3, Paris, Dec. 1931.

Maurice Sandoz & Salvador Dali, **The Maze,** Guilford Press, London, 1945.

Edi Lanners, **Illusionen,** Verlag C.J. Bucher, Lucerne & Frankfurt, 1973.

Paul Eluard, 'Les plus belles cartes postales', in **Minotaure,** no.3–4, Paris, 1933.

Romi, **Mythologie du sein,** J.-J. Pauvert, Paris, 1965.

Robert Fones, **Anthropomorphiks,** Coach House Press, Toronto, 1971.

Les Coleman, **The Jewish Banana,** Number Nineteen, London, 1973.

Illustrations

Acknowledgements

Christine Hammond (for our title), Philip Norman, David Sylvester, Doug Sandle, A. Leonard, John Lyle, Les Coleman, Brian Mills, John Jesse, Michael Tickner, Stephen Coe, Ian Breakwell, Sydney Graham, Christian Tobas, George Brecht, Darryl Francis, A. Ross Eckler, Glen Baxter, George Melly, Tony Earnshaw, Gerald Buchanan, Leslie Dunkling, Allen Jones, Trevor Winkfield, Iona and Peter Opie, Marcel Mariën, Jane Graverol, Nick Kimberley, John Timbers, Barbara Hulanicki, Jeff Edwards, Bryan Wynter, Mike Wallington, Philip Oakes, Alan F.G. Lewis, Robin and Carol Page, Valerie Monahan, Jack Sharratt, Rita Maran, John S. Crosbie, Christophe Harter, G. Chowdharay-Best, Nigel Vinson, Sandra McCosh, John A. Walker, George S. Green, James Hughes, Solomon Hughes, Molly Parkin, Clive Philpott, Eric Quayle, Ana Forcada, Diane Atkinson and especially to Hilary Rubinstein and Piers Dudgeon.

Especial thanks for this new edition to Kirsty Sellman, for sourcing imagery and to Jay Treagus for photography.

www.ingramcontent.com/pod-product-compliance
Ingram Content Group UK Ltd.
Pitfield, Milton Keynes, MK11 3LW, UK
UKHW021841240725
461145UK00012B/140

9 781915 580290